CRIME AND DETECTION

DOMESTIC CRIME

CRIME AND DETECTION

- Capital Punishment
- Criminal Terminology
- Cyber Crime
- Daily Prison Life
- Domestic Crime
- Famous Trials
- Forensic Science
- Global Terrorism
- Government Intelligence Agencies
- Hate Crimes
- The History of Punishment
- The History of Torture
- Infamous Prisons
- Organized Crime
- Protecting Yourself Against Criminals
- Race and Crime
- Serial Murders
- Unsolved Crimes
- The U.S. Justice System
- The War on Drugs

CRIME AND DETECTION

DOMESTIC CRIME

Isobel Brown

Foreword by Manny Gomez, Esq.

Dorr Township
1804 Sunset Dr.
LIBRARY
Dorr MI 49323
SURPLUS
DUPLICATE

MASON CREST

Mason Crest
450 Parkway Drive, Suite D
Broomall, PA 19008
www.masoncrest.com

Copyright © 2017 by Mason Crest, an imprint of National Highlights, Inc. All rights reserved. No part of this publication may be reproduced or transmitted in any form or by any means, electronic or mechanical, including photocopying, recording, taping, or any information storage and retrieval system, without permission in writing from the publisher.

Printed and bound in the United States of America

First printing
9 8 7 6 5 4 3 2 1

Series ISBN: 978-1-4222-3469-3
Hardcover ISBN: 978-1-4222-3474-7
ebook ISBN: 978-1-4222-8401-8

Library of Congress Cataloging-in-Publication Data on file with the Library of Congress

Developed and Produced by Print Matters Productions, Inc. (www.printmattersinc.com)

Developmental Editor: Amy Hackney Blackwell
Cover and Interior Design: Tom Carling, Carling Design Inc.

Note on Statistics: While every effort has been made to provide the most up-to-date government statistics, the Department of Justice and other agencies compile new data at varying intervals, sometimes as much as ten years. Agency publications are often based on data compiled from a period ending a year or two before the publication date.

CONTENTS

Foreword by Manny Gomez, Esq.	6
A Woman Scorned	11
The Angry Male	21
Trouble with Neighbors	33
Child Abuse	45
Child Criminals	55
Life After Crime	69
Series Glossary	83
Chronology	89
Further Information	91
Index	95
Picture Credits	96

KEY ICONS TO LOOK FOR:

Text-Dependent Questions: These questions send the reader back to the text for more careful attention to the evidence presented there.

Words to Understand: These words with their easy-to-understand definitions will increase the reader's understanding of the text while building vocabulary skills.

Series Glossary of Key Terms: This back-of-the-book glossary contains terminology used throughout this series. Words found here increase the reader's ability to read and comprehend higher-level books and articles in this field.

Research Projects: Readers are pointed toward areas of further inquiry connected to each chapter. Suggestions are provided for projects that encourage deeper research and analysis.

Sidebars: This boxed material within the main text allows readers to build knowledge, gain insights, explore possibilities, and broaden their perspectives by weaving together additional information to provide realistic and holistic perspectives.

FOREWORD

Experience Counts

Detecting crime and catching lawbreakers is a very human endeavor. Even the best technology has to be guided by human intelligence to be used effectively. If there's one truth from my thirty years in law enforcement and security, it's trust your gut.

When I started on the police force, I learned from older officers and from experience what things to look for, what traits, characteristics, or indicators lead to somebody who is about to commit a crime or in the process of committing one. You learn from experience. The older generation of law enforcement teaches the younger generation, and then, if you're good, you pick up your own little nuances as to what bad guys are doing.

In my early work, I specialized in human intelligence, getting informants to tell me what was happening on the street. Most of the time it was people I arrested that I then "flipped" to inform me where the narcotics were being stored, how they were being delivered, how they were being sold, the patterns, and other crucial details.

A good investigator has to be organized since evidence must be presented in a legally correct way to hold up in court. Evidence from a crime scene has to have a perfect chain of custody. Any mishandling turns the evidence to fruits of a poisonous tree.

At my company, MG Security Services, which provides private security to corporate and individual clients in the New York area, we are always trying to learn and to pass on that learning to our security officers in the field.

Certainly, the field of detection has evolved dramatically in the last 100 years. Recording devices have been around for a long time; it's just that now they've gotten really good. Today, a pen can be a video recording device; whereas in the old days it would have been a large box with two wheels. The equipment was awkward and not too subtle: it would be eighty degrees out, you'd be sweating in a raincoat, and the box would start clicking.

The forensic part of detection is very high-tech these days, especially with DNA coming into play in the last couple of decades. A hundred years ago, fingerprinting revolutionized detective work; the next breakthrough is facial recognition. We have recently discovered that the arrangement of facial features (measured as nodes) is unique to each individual. No two people on the planet have the exact same configuration of nodes. Just as it took decades to build out the database of known fingerprints, facial recognition is a work in progress. We will see increasing collection of facial data when people obtain official identification. There are privacy concerns, but we're working them out. Facial recognition will be a centerpiece of future detection and prevention efforts.

Technology offers law enforcement important tools that we're learning to apply strategically. Algorithms already exist that allow retailers to signal authorities when someone makes a suspicious purchase—known bomb-making ingredients, for example. Cities are loaded with sensors to detect the slightest trace of nuclear, biological, or chemical materials that pose a threat to the public. And equipment nested on streetlights in New York City can triangulate the exact block where a gun was fired.

Now none of this does anything constructive without well-trained professionals ready and able to put the information to use. The tools evolve, but what doesn't evolve is human intelligence.

Law enforcement as a community is way ahead in fighting street and violent crime than the newer challenges of cybercrime and terrorism. Technology helps, but it all goes back to human intelligence. There is no substitute for the cop on the street, knowing what is going on in the neighborhood, knowing who the players are. When the cop has quality informants inside gangs, he or she knows when there's going to be a hit, a drug drop, or an illicit transaction. The human intelligence comes first; then you can introduce the technology, such as hidden cameras or other surveillance.

The twin challenges for domestic law enforcement are gangs and guns. Gangs are a big problem in this country. That's a cultural and social phenomenon that law enforcement has not yet found an effective way to counteract. We need to study that more diligently. If we're successful in getting rid of the gangs, or at least diluting them, we will have come a long way in fighting violent crime. But guns are the main issue. You look at England, a first-world country of highly educated people that strictly regulates guns, and the murder rate is minimal.

When it comes to cybercrime, we're woefully behind. That's simply because we hire people for the long term, and their skills get old. You have a twenty-five-year-old who's white-hot now, but guess what? In five years that skill set is lost. Hackers, on the other hand, are young people who tend to evolve fast. They learn so much more than their older law-enforcement counterparts and are able to penetrate systems too easily. The Internet was not built with the security of private users in mind. It is like a house with no door locks, and now we're trying to figure ways to secure the house. It was done kind of backward. Nobody really thought that it was going to be this wide-open door to criminal activity.

We need to change the equation for cybercriminals. Right now the chances are they won't get caught; cybercrime offers criminals huge benefit at very little cost. Law enforcement needs to recruit young people who can match skills with the criminals. We also need to work closely with foreign governments and agencies to better identify, deter, and apprehend cybercriminals. We need to make examples of them.

Improving our cybercrime prevention means a lot more talent, a lot more resources, a lot more hands-on collaboration with countries on the outskirts—Russia, China, even Israel. These are the countries that are constantly trying to penetrate our cyberspace. And even if we are able to identify the person overseas, we still need the cooperation of the overseas government and law enforcement to help us find and apprehend the person. Electrical grids are extremely vulnerable to cyber attacks. Utilities built long before the Internet need engineering retrofits to make them better able to withstand attacks.

As with cybercrime, efforts against terrorism must be coordinated to be effective. Communication is crucial among all levels of law enforcement, from local law enforcement and national agencies sharing information—in both directions—to a similar international flow of information among different countries' governments and national bureaus.

In the U.S., since 9/11, the FBI and local law enforcement now share a lot more information with each other locally and nationally. Internationally, as well, we are sharing more information with Interpol and other intelligence and law enforcement agencies throughout the world to be able to better detect, identify, and prevent criminal activity.

When it comes to terrorism, we also need to ramp up our public relations. Preventing terror attacks takes more than a military response. We need to address this culture of death with our own Internet media campaign and 800 numbers to make it easy for people to reach out to law enforcement and help build the critical human infrastructure. Without people, there are no leads—people on the inside of a criminal enterprise are essential to directing law enforcement resources effectively, telling you when to listen, where to watch, and which accounts to check.

In New York City, the populace is well aware of the "see something, say something" campaign. Still, we need to do more. More people need to speak up. Again, it comes down to trusting your instincts. If someone seems a little off to you, find a law enforcement representative and share your perception. Listen to your gut. Your gut will always tell you: there's something hinky going on here. Human beings have a sixth sense that goes back to our caveman days when animals used to hunt us. So take action, talk to law enforcement when something about a person makes you uneasy or you feel something around you isn't right.

We have to be prepared not just on the prevention side but in terms of responses. Almost every workplace conducts a fire drill at least once a year. We need to do the same with active-shooter drills. Property managers today may even have their own highly trained active-shooter teams, ready to be on site within minutes of any attack.

We will never stop crime, but we can contain the harm it causes. The coordinated efforts of law enforcement, an alert and well-trained citizenry, and the smart use of DNA, facial profiles, and fingerprinting will go a long way toward reducing the number and severity of terror events.

Be it the prevention of street crime or cybercrime, gang violence or terrorism, sharing information is essential. Only then can we put our technology to good use. People are key to detection and prevention. Without the human element, I like to say a camera's going to take a pretty picture of somebody committing a crime.

Law enforcement must strive to attract qualified people with the right instincts, team-sensibility, and work ethic. At the end of the day, there's no hunting like the hunting of man. It's a thrill; it's a rush; and that to me is law enforcement in its purest form.

MANNY GOMEZ, Esq.

President of MG Security Services,

Chairman of the National Law Enforcement Association,

former FBI Special Agent,

U.S. Marine, and NYPD Sergeant

CRIME AND DETECTION

DOMESTIC CRIME

CHAPTER 1

A WOMAN SCORNED

Words to Understand

Infidelity: unfaithfulness, often during marriage

Manslaughter: the unlawful killing of a human being without express or implied intent

Motive: reason for a certain course of action whether conscious or unconscious

Premeditated: characterized by fully conscious willful intent and a measure of forethought and planning

DOMESTIC CRIME STARTED WITH THE BEGINNING OF HUMAN RELATIONSHIPS. THERE HAS NEVER BEEN A TIME WHEN STRESS WITHIN FAMILIES OR BETWEEN COUPLES HAS NOT BEEN KNOWN TO FLARE OUT OF CONTROL, RESULTING IN VIOLENCE AND MURDER. WHEREVER YOU LOOK—IN HISTORY, RELIGION, OR LITERATURE—THERE ARE DYSFUNCTIONAL FAMILIES WHERE PASSION AND FURY HAS OVERTAKEN REASON AND SOMEONE HAS KILLED.

The story of Cain killing Abel still catches the imagination today. The tale has become a parable for the most terrible of crimes—murdering a close family member in a fit of jealousy. Every minute about 20 people are physically abused by an intimate partner in the United States, according the Centers for Disease Control and Prevention.

In the Bible, Cain, the elder son of Adam and Eve, killed his brother Abel and became the world's first murderer, thus setting a pattern for disastrous family relationships where jealousy and hatred can spiral out of control. Cain had long been resentful that his work in the fields was not appreciated, while the achievements of Abel the shepherd were praised. When his objections were brushed aside, Cain was left feeling undervalued, jealous, and angry. He brooded, and one day he killed. The emotions that drove him to it have been familiar **motives** for violence ever since.

When "Home" Is Not a Haven

Only about 16 percent of murder victims in the United States are killed by total strangers. About 30 percent are killed by relatives, and another 54 percent by friends, neighbors, boyfriends, and others they know fairly well. In the case of female murder victims, 35 percent are killed by husbands or boyfriends. For every person who is killed, there are thousands more who are subjected to physical violence at home. Victims and attackers alike are found in every walk of life and in every age group. Sadly, for too many people, their home is not the haven of love and comfort that it ought to be.

Until recently, violence between couples in the home has often gone unreported. Today, however, as the scale of the problem has come to light, organizations have been set up to tackle the issue.

Many people believe that women are less threatening and more restrained than men, a belief that makes the physical attacks they commit seem more shocking. When Lorena Bobbit cut off her sleeping husband's penis, she was taking her revenge for his marital **infidelity**. Inadvertently, the American housewife was also making herself notorious as the woman who acted out every male's nightmare; and she was sending out a general warning that women can be vicious, too.

Women kill far less often than men and represent only 1.5 percent of the prisoners on Death Row in the United States. Unlike men, women rarely have sexual or financial motives for murder. And there are no known cases of a woman abusing and killing a child unless a man was involved, too.

So could Rudyard Kipling, the Victorian writer, possibly have got it right in that much-quoted line, "The female of the species is more deadly than the male"? Certainly, the courts everywhere have often behaved as if it is true. For example, in the U.K. in the 1980s, it emerged that when men and women were convicted of equally serious crimes of violence, the women were generally given longer sentences, partly because of the perception that violence by a woman was worse. However, there was also a legal problem for women defendants arising from the fact that men and women commit violent crimes in different ways.

Discrimination in the Legal System

A man who lashed out at his nagging wife on the spur of the moment and killed her was unlikely to be convicted of murder. He could plead provocation as a defense, meaning he had suffered a momentary lapse of reason and had acted irrationally for a terrible second. Yet for a woman who had endured physical cruelty for years, and eventually killed her abuser while he was asleep or drunk, the provocation defense would rarely succeed because her act was deemed **premeditated**. The simple fact that a woman is too weak to kill a man with her hands and has to fetch a weapon has been used to prove premeditation. After much debate and a few well-publicized cases—including that of Sara Thornton, given a lengthy prison sentence when she killed after years of abuse—it is increasingly accepted that legal systems discriminate against women charged with murdering men.

This change of attitude has led to a bid to overturn the murder conviction of Ruth Ellis, the last woman to be executed in the U.K. A London prostitute and nightclub manager, she was 28 when she was hanged on July 13, 1955, for killing her racing-driver lover, David Blakely. He had left her, but she traced him to the Magdala public house in London and, as he walked out into the street one April afternoon that year, she shot him dead with a Smith and Wesson. They had been together for several turbulent years. In 1953, she had had an abortion and he

With this borrowed Smith and Wesson, Ruth Ellis murdered her lover. A revolver was a rare weapon for a woman, especially in 1950s London. But there were many guns in circulation at the time, because men had failed to hand in service revolvers after World War II.

offered to marry her, but Ellis, with an illegitimate daughter and a failed marriage behind her, decided to end the relationship. Blakely, highly emotional, would not let her go, and by 1955, they were living together, although she was seeing other lovers, and he began drinking heavily. After a short trial, the jury took barely 14 minutes to find her guilty of murder. It was a disquieting case that led many more people to support the abolition of the death penalty.

Sara Thornton leaves Oxford Crown Court during her retrial. Her original murder conviction, for stabbing her abusive husband, was quashed because her personality disorder had not been considered. At the retrial, she was sentenced to five years for **manslaughter**.

Ruth Ellis

The Ruth Ellis story was dramatized in 1985 in a sympathetic movie, *Dance With A Stranger* starring Miranda Richardson, which showed how the relationship between Ellis and her lover altered until David Blakely ceased to be dependent on her, but she was desperate to hold on to him. In this mood, and suffering the effects of a miscarriage, she shot him.

Fifty years after her execution, Ruth Ellis's family campaigned to have her conviction reduced to manslaughter on the grounds of her diminished mental responsibility. The Criminal Cases Review Commission referred it to the Appeal Court in February 2002. It was unusual for the Commission to refer a case where the issue was not a matter of guilt or innocence. At her trial, there had been no doubt about her guilt. Asked about her intention when she fired the gun, she replied, "I intended to kill him."

On the eve of her execution, Ellis wrote a statement identifying a man who had given her the gun and driven her to the Magdala public house. The police were not shown it for 25 years, and the man they then interviewed denied involvement.

Whatever the precise circumstances of her personal tragedy, the Ruth Ellis story bears the hallmarks of the typical case of a rejected woman turning killer in any country and at any time in history: a soured relationship, obsession, passion turned to anger, and a need to punish and destroy. Emotional energy redirected to seeking revenge is deadly.

The Murder of Dr. Tarnower

Even if it is true that, as English playwright and poet William Congreve put it, "Hell hath no fury like a woman scorned," most women who take action stop long before causing serious harm, contenting themselves by destroying the lover's possessions or humiliating him. A middle-aged writer, who publicly threw beer over her husband and his mistress before lobbing bricks through their window, described herself as "euphoric with rage." By the time she started flinging things, she had decided to file for divorce. What was in the mind of Jean Harris when she shot Dr. Herman Tarnower was less clear. A jury took eight days to find her guilty of second-degree murder, and she was sentenced to 15 years.

The killing, in March 1980, was a sensation because Dr. Tarnower was an eminent cardiologist and famous as the inventor of the Scarsdale Diet. Jean Harris, 57, was headmistress of a private school for girls in Virginia. For 14 years, the pair had been lovers until Tarnower, 69, switched his affections to a younger woman who worked in his office. Depressed, Harris wrote her will and put it with a .32 revolver in her bag before making the five-hour drive to his Westchester home. She arrived late, awoke Tarnower, and soon shots were fired. His housekeeper found him lying wounded on the floor in Harris's arms.

Jean Harris always insisted the shooting was an accident, saying she planned to die herself, but when she showed the gun, there was a tussle and he was shot instead. However, during the four-month trial, the prosecution revealed a letter, described as a devastating catalog of bitterness and resentment, in which she attacked Tarnower and the woman who had supplanted her. The prosecution painted a picture of Harris in a jealous rage, ripping clothes and throwing things, before producing the gun. Thirty live rounds of ammunition in her car did not suggest suicide, they argued.

The defense claimed Harris had been in a disturbed state because she was suffering withdrawal symptoms after going without methamphetamine for several days. This powerful

Dr. Herman Tarnower, renowned cardiologist and creator of the Scarsdale Diet.

stimulant is known to have mind-altering side effects if taken over a long period. Dr. Tarnower, the jury was told, had been prescribing it for her for 10 years.

Marry or Be Murdered

The body of a successful American businessman lay in his blood-soaked bedroom in London one weekend in the summer of 2000 while the woman he had refused to marry went on the run. Jane Andrews, 34, former assistant to the Duchess of York, had smashed him with a cricket bat and stabbed him twice with an eight-inch kitchen knife. The day before he died, Thomas Cressman had told the police he and Andrews were arguing and he was afraid someone was going to get hurt. On Monday, when he did not show up at work, one of his employees went to the home the couple shared in Fulham, southwest London. Once the body was examined, the police search for Andrews began.

Detectives asked friends and family to try and reach her on her cell phone, and the Duchess left two messages urging, "You must come forward and help the police." However, Andrews replied that she did not know why people were contacting her because everything was fine when she left home. Four days later, she told another friend she was in Cornwall (in southwest England) and had attempted suicide by taking an overdose of painkillers. Police found her by the roadside, living in her car.

Andrews had worked as a royal aide for nine years, a glamorous life for a joiner's daughter from the northern English town of Cleethorpes. When she was 21, she answered an anonymous advertisement in a magazine called *The Lady* for a personal dresser, and that was the start of jet-setting, organizing the duchess's wardrobe, managing her accounts, and shopping for her. It was Jane Andrews who was responsible for the safety of the royal jewelry when a diamond necklace and bracelet worth £250,000 ($400,000) were stolen on a flight in 1995. The Duchess, amused at her assistant's new refined accent and changed manner, dubbed her Lady Jane.

Andrews became obsessed with the Duchess and was devastated when she was fired in 1997. No other job could equal the one she had lost. Tom Cressman, however, with his money and society contacts, was a link to her lost world. The son of Palm Beach millionaires Harry and Barbara Cressman, Tom loved fast cars, vintage boats, and the bachelor life. But Andrews, now 34 and craving marriage and children, convinced herself he would propose while they were on vacation in Italy and France. Instead, he told her he had no intention of marrying someone whose jealousy and possessiveness were always causing trouble. They returned to London and a weekend of arguments that culminated in murder.

Statistics on Domestic Crime

The National Crime Victimization Survey published by the U.S. Department of Justice is the primary source of information on criminal victimization in the United States. Each year, it takes data from 50,000 households on the frequency, characteristics, and consequences of crime. The DOJ also publishes data on homicides in the United States. The Centers for Disease Control and Prevention's (CDC) National Intimate Partner and Sexual Violence Survey is another good source of data specifically on sexual assaults.

- In 2011, over half the victims of rapes and sexual assaults said the attacker was an intimate (meaning a current or former spouse, a boyfriend, or girlfriend) or a relative, friend, or other acquaintance.
- Women more commonly suffer violence at the hands of intimates, while men are more likely to be attacked by strangers. Intimates were responsible for 748,800 violent assaults on women in 2013, down from 1,031,720 in 2004.
- In 2009, almost 80 percent of murder victims were slain by family members, boyfriends, friends, and acquaintances. As of 2012, of the women murdered, 34 percent were killed by intimate partners; only 2.5 percent of male victims were killed by their intimate partners. The most common murder method is shooting with a gun.
- At least half of female sexual assault victims (the percentage varies depending on the particular assault) know their assailants. Among women who are stalked, about 84 percent are stalked by a family member, an acquaintance, or a current or former partner. The CDC estimates that some 22 percent of women experience at least one instance of severe physical violence by an intimate partner during their lives.

Unlike Ruth Ellis, who admitted intending to kill David Blakely, and unlike Jean Harris, who maintained she killed Dr. Tarnower by accident, Jane Andrews tried to shift the blame. She betrayed Tom Cresswell, claiming he had been a violent partner, killed in self-defense after raping and threatening to kill her. However, the forensic evidence at the bloody scene of the crime was witness to her savagery, and it was her own character, not that of the victim, that was destroyed as her story came apart under cross-examination. After she was sentenced to life, one former boyfriend described how she had stalked him and another told how she vandalized his apartment when he had ended their affair.

Jane Andrews and Tom Cressman pose for a photograph. Sentencing her to life, the judge said, "In killing the man you loved, you ended his life and ruined your own. It is evident that you made your attack when you were consumed with anger and bitterness. Nothing could justify what you did."

Text-Dependent Questions

1. What is domestic violence?
2. Are men or women more likely to commit domestic crimes?
3. If a woman is murdered, is she most likely to have been killed by a stranger or by someone she knows?

Research Projects

1. Find statistics on domestic violence in your state. Who are the most common victims? What types of assaults are most common?
2. What sort of personality traits lead men to abuse women? Is abuse evenly spread through all communities or is it concentrated in certain groups?
3. What can a victim of domestic violence do about her (or his) situation? What resources are available to help?

CHAPTER 2
THE ANGRY MALE

Words to Understand

Absolute monarch: a king or queen with total power

Acrimony: harsh words, manner, or disposition

Alibi: a defense by an accused person that he was elsewhere when a crime was committed

Acquit: to discharge completely from an accusation

Parliament: assembly of representatives of the people, which is often the supreme legislative authority

Parole: release before the end of a sentence on condition of continuing good conduct

ONE OF THE MOST ASTONISHING ACTS OF DOMESTIC VIOLENCE OCCURRED IN THE ROYAL PALACE IN KATHMANDU, NEPAL, IN 2001. CROWN PRINCE DIPENDRA, THE 29-YEAR-OLD HEIR TO THE THRONE, SLAUGHTERED 14 OF HIS FAMILY.

Clad in battle dress and armed with several guns, including an Ml6 assault rifle, Crown Prince Dipendra entered the drawing room where his family had gathered after dinner and began firing. As they lay dead and dying, he shot himself. By the time he was declared dead two days later, the tiny Himalayan country was in turmoil, its monarchy tottering. Officials were finally forced to admit that the massacre was not a political act by a faction attempting to overthrow the royal family, but a domestic murder by the heir to the throne. This was especially appalling because in the Hindu religion of Nepal, the king is a demigod, the reincarnation of Lord Vishnu.

Women and children are often in the greatest danger from male members of their own family. Studies in the United States found that 40–60 percent of mothers of 32 abused children were also victimized by their partners.

Violence Toward Women

Most domestic murders are at the opposite end of the scale. Usually, a man kills his wife or girlfriend. Margaret Atwood, the Canadian writer, pinpointed a truth when she said, "Men fear being laughed at by women. Women fear being killed by men." Women also fear being raped and beaten. Because it has become more common for women to report incidents of physical abuse to the police, an alarming level of violence has been revealed. There are four million cases of domestic abuse against women annually in the United States. One out of four emergency visits to hospitals in the United States are made by women as a result of domestic assaults.

Domestic violence is a worldwide problem, and many countries now have initiatives to tackle it. This poster, depicting an aggressive male beating his wife while a child tries to restrain him, was used in Phnom Penh, Cambodia, to publicize the issue.

Nearly all women experience domestic violence at some stage of their lives, according to CDC statistics from 2011. Women who stay at home are more likely to become victims than women who go out to work. If a wife relies on her husband for financial support, either by choice or through unemployment, she runs a higher risk of physical harm than a woman in an equal partnership. The survey revealed that men who believed in male dominance and held patriarchal attitudes were more likely to think beating their wives was legitimate. Researchers described the attitudes of young boys toward domestic violence and its perpetrators as "worryingly tolerant."

Mass Murder in the Name of Romance

Crown Prince Dipendra (pictured) had been known to be unhappy with his lack of control over his life. As one of his uncles said later, he was torn apart by being a medieval monarch in a modern world. Survivors agreed that it was an argument with his mother over his parents' implacable opposition to him marrying the woman he loved, Devyana Rana, that ignited his murderous rage that evening. King Birendra and Queen Aishwarya had educated their son at Eton College in England, but when in Nepal, he was required to lead a life ordered by Nepalese tradition. Against Dipendra's wishes, his father had legalized political parties and accepted a **parliamentary** system. This meant that when Dipendra succeeded to the throne, he would not be an **absolute monarch**, but rather the figurehead of a constitutional monarchy. There were those at court who had long warned that the crown prince was psychologically unfit to become a king. In any event, he was proclaimed king on his deathbed and was succeeded by his uncle.

The picture in other countries is similar, and in recent years, a number have mounted campaigns to reduce the abuse of women. The U.S. Department of Justice's Office on Violence against Women handles domestic violence, sexual assault, and stalking in the United States. It provides grants to help states, tribes, and local communities transform the ways in which criminal justice systems respond to these events. There are also government-funded programs to help men learn to control aggression. Anger-management programs for overaggressive males, within prisons and in the community, are increasingly common.

High-profile cases involving celebrities, such as OJ. Simpson or Mike Tyson, have raised public awareness of the problem of violence toward women. Retired football player Simpson was found not guilty when he was tried for the 1995 murders of his ex-wife Nicole Brown, with whom he had had a violent relationship, and her new partner Ronald Goldman. However, in a later action, brought by the victims' families, a civil court found that he was involved. Damages were awarded against him–$25 million to be shared between Nicole's children and Goldman's father.

Boxer Mike Tyson has a history of violent outbursts, including domestic violence during his brief marriage to actress Robin Givens. In 1992, he was sentenced to six years for raping a Miss Black America contestant, Desiree Washington, 18, in his hotel room.

Ex-partners Who Stalk

Women are also increasingly the victims of stalkers. Although the most publicized cases feature celebrities, these are a small minority. According to the CDC, as of 2011 an estimated 15.2 percent of women had experienced stalking that made them fearful. About 88.3 percent were stalked only by males; they knew about 84 percent of their stalkers.

OJ. Simpson was tried for double murder in one of the most highly publicized and bitterly contested murder trials of all time. Millions of Americans witnessed his **acquittal** on live television.

Boxer Mike Tyson was the youngest ever heavyweight champion, yet his violent behavior has resulted in imprisonment. Many commentators point to his traumatic childhood as a reason for his abusive outbursts, but bad childhood experiences do not necessarily lead to violence in later life.

John Johnson has stalked pop star Madonna for more than 10 years, bombarding her with love letters, flowers, and chocolates. New laws in the U.S. and U.K. have been implemented to stop this kind of obsessive and frightening behavior.

When the Victorian Institute of Forensic Mental Health in Melbourne, Australia, undertook one of the most comprehensive studies of stalkers to date, the results they published in the *American Journal of Psychiatry* showed that 80 percent were men and a third were ex-partners of their victims. In London, a group of psychiatrists from the Royal Free Hospital and Chase Farm Hospital, led by Dr. Frank Farnham, reported in *The Lancet,* "The greatest danger of serious violence from stalkers is not from strangers or from people with psychotic illness, but from non-psychotic ex-partners." Ex-partners who stalked resorted to serious violence in 70 percent of the cases studied, while strangers did so in 27 percent.

The crimes of Anthony Hurdle, sentenced to life after pleading guilty to attempting to murder Lorraine Nicholson, illustrate the terrible consequences when a man refuses to accept the end of a relationship. Lorraine Nicholson learned from a television documentary that the man in her life was "Britain's most notorious stalker," and she broke up with him. Hurdle, a former naval officer previously known as Anthony Burstow, had begun stalking in 1993 by following, phoning, and sending obscene letters to an earlier girlfriend, Tracey Sant. He served three prison sentences for burgling Sant's home, stealing her underwear, following her, and littering her front yard with condoms. In 1996, he was jailed for three years for causing grievous bodily harm to her mind, a case that attracted much attention because it was a test of the courts' new powers in stalking cases.

After Lorraine Nicholson dropped Hurdle, he became obsessed with her and began stalking again. On one occasion, he forced his way through the front door of her home in Ashford, Kent, and slashed her arm with such force that her hand was almost completely severed.

I Will Find You and I Will Kill You

Domestic murder cases that clutch the public attention are often those in which the victim seemed to have it all: physical beauty, enviable lifestyle, career success, good health, happy family, and loyal friends. Then suddenly disaster strikes, and the curtain of privacy is torn aside to reveal the innermost secrets of a life as police investigate and the press ferret out the details. There is no discretion in a murder case, no privacy for the dead and none for those close to the victim.

The murder plot that ended the life of Sheila Bellush was a headline-catcher. She had led a glamorous life as the wife of Allen Blackthorne, a young Texas millionaire who had made his fortune selling medical equipment. Then, in 1987, she had him arrested for beating her up. They divorced, but the **acrimony** continued. Sheila met and married Jamie Bellush, won custody of her two daughters, and gave birth to quadruplets. Then the Bellush family moved 1,200 miles away to Sarasota, Florida.

Violence in the home is much more common than many people are prepared to admit. In the United States, there are four million cases of domestic abuse against women annually, almost all perpetrated by men.

Texas millionaire Allen Blackthorne was sentenced to life imprisonment without parole for paying $50,000 to have his ex-wife murdered.

Every Breath You Take

In a final dramatic twist to the tragic story of Sheila Bellush, Ann Rule, author of several books based on crimes in the United States, has written about the case in *Every Breath You Take*. This time, she was writing at the request of the victim because, believing her life in danger from Blackthorne, Sheila Bellush had written, asking Rule to do so should she be murdered.

Blackthorne hired a private investigator to trace Sheila, a task that proved difficult, but he persisted. Three weeks after Blackthorne managed to obtain her address, Sheila was murdered at home.

Her eldest daughter, Stevie, aged 15, found her in the laundry room, shot in the face and with her throat slashed. The babies lay unharmed beside her. Stevie

The Angry Male   27

told the police immediately that she believed her father was responsible for the murder of her mother.

Police found ample evidence at the scene: a fingerprint, a knife, a bullet shell, and neighbors who had noticed the Texas license plate of a car driven by a suspicious-looking man. The man they traced was Jose Luis del Toro. As the plot unraveled, investigators found that all strands led to Blackthorne. Blackthorne's golfing buddy, Danny Rocha, had hired del Toro and others to kill Sheila Bellush. Blackthorne had paid Rocha to organize the killing. Rocha and Blackthorne had played golf together at the time of the murder to give each other **alibis**.

Prosecutors at Allen Blackthorne's trial portrayed him as a man obsessed with his ex-wife and full of hate, willing to pay $50,000 to have her killed. Most damning, their chief witness was his golfing buddy, convicted at an earlier hearing for his part in the crime. Rocha's evidence confirmed Blackthorne as the financier and mastermind of the murder plot. The trial judge sentenced Blackthorne to life imprisonment without **parole**.

Overwhelming Passion

Sensational details lift a murder story from the typical to the intriguing and newsworthy, but every case is marked by overwhelming passion. Often, the victim has made an effort to improve her life and seen it go wrong, or she is blinded by love for a dangerous man. All this happened to Julie Scully.

Julie Scully had the beautiful face of her Navaho mother: almond-shaped brown eyes and high cheekbones. She became a popular newspaper pin-up and model in New Jersey. She was intelligent and worked hard, determined to have the independence of a career while continuing to work as office manager in her millionaire husband's landscaping business. Then, inexplicably, she fell under the spell of a Greek sailor during a vacation cruise and sacrificed everything, including her life.

George Skiadopolous, who had a history of violent attacks on family members, murdered her in Greece once he guessed she was not going to marry him. When his attempt to cover up the crime failed, he led police to her body in a lake, but it was a body minus a head. He went on trial for murder and desecrating a body, and was sentenced to life without parole.

Julie Scully grew up headstrong and hot-tempered, angry with a beat-cop father who left home on her ninth birthday and a violent mother addicted to alcohol and drugs. At 17, seeking emotional and financial security, she married a man six years older than herself. Aged 21, she met her second husband, Tim Nist, a New Jersey businessman 11 years her senior. Nist encouraged her modeling, and soon she was the most popular "Page Six girl" in *The Trentonian,* busy promoting the newspaper at charity softball games, parades, and on television. Modeling and partying, she was in her element. When the birth of her daughter Katie meant a pause in her work, she grew depressed and started using drugs.

The couple took a short Caribbean cruise on the *Galaxy,* Celebrity Cruises' new flagship liner. Julie caught the eye of the third engineer. Her gold jewelry signaled to Skiadopolous that she was rich as well as beautiful, and he began to seduce her. Desperate to see him again, she took her husband on the cruise for a second time and later flew to meet the ship in port. Her passion for Skiadopolous had become everything.

Third engineer George Skiadopoious puts a protective arm around Scully as they pose for a photograph taken by her husband during a holiday cruise in the Caribbean. Blinded by her passion for the young Greek, she lost everything, including her life.

The Angry Male

Violence in the American Home

- Three women die every day at the hands of their husbands and boyfriends—approximately 1,400 women a year. Between 2003 and 2011, about 18,000 women were killed by men in domestic disputes.

- About 4,700,00 women are battered each year. About 38,000,000 women have experience physical violence from intimate partners over their lifetimes. Women with disabilities are 40 percent more likely to experience violence from partners. The risk of murder is 70 times higher in the weeks just after a woman leaves an abusive partner than at other times.

- One-third of the women surveyed by the CDC in 2011 reported that they had been victims of rape, beating, or stalking. The CDC estimates that 1.3 million American women are the victims of rape or attempted rape each year.

- The main reason women stay with their abusive partners is money; their abusers control their finances.

The New Man Tightens His Hold

Once Tim Nist and Julie parted, Skiadopolous tightened his hold, moving in with her, banning her from working, and keeping her friends and family away. Everyone knew she was deluded, but nobody could convince her that the affair was certain to end badly. To them, he was unattractive and dangerous and definitely after her money. Yet in Julie's eyes, he could do no wrong, despite the fact that he was clearly a violent man—he had once even tried to strangle Julie's mother.

He was unable to remain legally in the United States, so they moved to his hometown of Kavala, 400 miles north of Athens. Before her possessions had even arrived, her romantic dreams faded. His family rejected her as a divorcee who had left a child behind, an intolerable state of affairs for traditional Greek people. She hated the contrast between round-the-clock New Jersey and a Greek harbor town where bars closed for winter, but when she said so, he assaulted her. Afraid at last, she made secret plans to go home. Julie believed her chance would come when they went to Athens, supposedly to get married.

Skiadopolous, however, realized his scheme to marry an American and lead a comfortable life in the United States had foundered. Rather than set her free, he killed her on the road to Athens.

Days later, he reported her missing near a McDonald's in Omonia Square. When he telephoned her friends in New Jersey with his make-believe story, they suspected he had murdered her. They urged the American embassy and police in Athens and the United States to treat her disappearance seriously; they tracked spending on her accounts; and they consulted two psychics, who both described her body in water.

Pressure from her friends thrust the story of Julie Scully and her ruinous passion for the young sailor onto news pages and television programs in the United States and Greece. Within days of the story appearing in the press, Skiadopolous went to a police station to confess. He described strangling her, trying to burn the body, and then sawing off the head to cram the rest into a suitcase. The case was raised, but the head, which he claimed he threw from cliffs into the sea, was never found.

Text-Dependent Questions

1. What crimes do men commit against the women they live with?
2. What are some risk factors for domestic abuse?
3. How many women in the United States are battered by their husbands every year?

Research Projects

1. Choose a court case involving domestic abuse. What happened in this case? How was it resolved?
2. Research violence against women worldwide. Are some countries particularly prone to cases of domestic violence? Why might this be the case?
3. What is a stalker? Find an example of a case involving a stalker; research what happened. Why is stalking so hard on its victims?

The Angry Male

CHAPTER 3

TROUBLE WITH NEIGHBORS

Words to Understand

Antagonism: enmity or hostility
Maul: to wound by scratching or tearing
Obscene: offending morality and decency

PEOPLE CHOOSE THEIR FRIENDS, BUT THEY GET STUCK WITH THEIR NEIGHBORS. EVEN IF THEY CHECK THEM OUT BEFORE DECIDING TO BUY OR RENT A PLACE, THE SITUATION CAN CHANGE FOR THE WORSE. FRICTION BETWEEN NEIGHBORS CAN ARISE OVER THE PETTIEST THINGS, WHICH IS WHAT HAPPENS WHEN HUMAN BEINGS ARE OBLIGED TO LIVE CLOSE TO SOMEONE WHOSE PERSONALITY OR HABITS THEY DISLIKE. USUALLY, THE ISSUES ARE KEPT IN PROPORTION AND NOBODY ENDURES MORE THAN IRRITATION. OCCASIONALLY, HOWEVER, THE IRRITATION BECOMES A GRUDGE AND THE GRUDGE DEVELOPS INTO AN OBSESSION. WHEN THAT HAPPENS, IT FREQUENTLY ENDS IN CRIMINAL ACTS.

Marjorie Knoller clasp her hands together as evidence is presented in a courtroom in Los Angeles in March 2002. Her dogs had mauled a neighbor, Diane Whipple, to death. Knoller's husband was also convicted in a case that highlighted the dangers posed by neighbors' pets.

To outsiders, battling neighbors seem absurd. They regress to juvenile behavior to make life difficult for the "enemy"; they refuse to "give in," and a small matter that could have been settled by discussion and compromise escalates until it dominates their lives and those of their families.

Bad Neighbors Can Make You Sick

The case of the croaking plastic frogs amused newspaper readers, but Catherine Watt, 65, and her husband, James, 66, told a court in Glasgow, Scotland, that the constant noise coming from the next-door garden had made life a misery. Andrew Cromar, 39, was fined for causing annoyance. He had fitted four battery-operated garden ornaments with sensors to detect movement and placed them where they croaked nonstop day and night. When Mr. and Mrs. Watts complained about the obvious disturbance this was causing, he actually increased the number of artificial frogs, and when the police told him to switch them off, he refused.

A survey, carried out by Community Mediation, has shown that stress caused by quarreling with a neighbor can to lead to illnesses, such as the sleep disorder and high blood pressure reported by Mrs. Watt. Those already ill suffer increased heart trouble, strokes, and asthma.

Sometimes, an intimidating neighbor is less easy to detect. Poison pen letters or a spate of silent telephone calls makes the recipient suspicious of everyone. Unless physical harm is threatened or the telephone calls are **obscene**, the police are unlikely to intervene. The crimes of a pensioner in Caldicot, Wales, went undetected for 18 months. While Elaine Meredith, 62, was out walking her dog, she scratched obscenities on cars. Police suspected a gang of youths until a car owner caught her red-handed. She denied everything, even though forensics proved there was car paint on the knife in her coat pocket. She was sentenced to six months in prison.

A few miles away, at Abergavenny, a 75-year-old widow was conducting a war that culminated in death threats against her neighbors' baby. When she was convicted of harassment, a restraining order was imposed to prevent further intimidation of the Edwards family who lived next door. A year later, Evans was found guilty of seven breaches of the order, including verbal abuse, striking a car with her broom, and making threatening gestures. Passing a prison sentence of nine months, suspended for two years because of her medical condition, Judge David Morris told her, "You are a manipulative and vindictive old woman who clearly harassed your neighbors. You are the original neighbor from hell." And he warned the Edwards family that the court had no powers to prevent her from going straight back home.

Dangerous Pets

Neighbors who keep dangerous animals are especially threatening. The owners of two Presa Canario mastiffs, which **mauled** a San Francisco neighbor, were convicted of murder, the first time that dog owners have been convicted of murder because of the action of their pets. Marjorie Knoller faced a prison sentence of 15 years for murdering Diane Whipple. Along with her husband, Robert Noel, she was also convicted of manslaughter and owning a mischievous animal that killed. Knoller and Noel, both lawyers and both associated with the Aryan Brotherhood, were caring for the dogs, Bane and Hera, which belonged to their adopted son who was serving a prison term. Thirty people from the neighborhood testified that the dogs had lunged and growled at them, and one man had even been bitten.

This dog is a pit bull terrier, one of many breeds of dog that have a reputation for attacking humans. According to the CDC, about 4.5 million dog bites occur each year in the United States. Thirty-nine people died of dog bites in 2013, but 20 percent of victims required medical attention, and 27,000 required reconstructive surgery. Children ages 5 to 9 are at highest risk. Most bites occur at home, with pet dogs.

Trouble with Neighbors

Diane Whipple, 33, a lacrosse coach, was trying to enter her apartment in Pacific Heights in January 2001 when they attacked. Bane, a 120-pound male, tore her throat out, while Hera, a 113-pound female, ripped her clothes. Knoller claimed she had tried to pull them off. After the killing, Diane Whipple's partner, Sharon Smith, campaigned for new state laws allowing same-sex partners to sue for wrongful death. As well as highlighting sexual and racial politics, the case focused on the widespread existence of neo-Nazi groups in prisons. The dogs, described in court as "time bombs, more dangerous than loaded guns," had been linked to a dog-fighting ring run from Pelican Bay State Prison.

Neighbors From Hell

Eli Street in Tucson, Arizona, was like any other suburban street in America: not rich, but respectable; no Beverly Hills, but a pleasant place to live. Up until the early 1990s, its residents considered themselves lucky to live there: then their lives were made utterly wretched by some true-life "neighbors from hell."

The trouble, says *Tucson Weekly*'s Vicki Hart, all seemed to center on just two households: the first was full of yelling, mischief-making children. Not just Teresa Embry's own five sons, left unsupervised day and night while she was out at work, but all the others who congregated in what had come to be the "neighborhood hangout." Car wrecks and other rubbish littered the front yard, making the house both an eyesore and a public-health menace. The other focal point for trouble was the house where Gregory Lindsey lived, along with his girlfriend Lisa and their little daughter, plus two teenage sons from his former marriage, in what appeared to be the very depths of domestic misery. One might have sympathized with Lindsey and Lisa if they did not drag their dirtiest linen out into the public eye, frequently fighting noisily and violently in the street before the eyes of the whole street. Meanwhile, Lindsey's sons appeared to have entered into competition with Teresa Embry's children to see who could cause the greatest nuisance in the shortest time.

The noise and disturbance never let up, with everything from loud music to gunfire around the clock, at any time of the day or night, but the trouble did not end there, by any means. The list of offenses committed in this once-quiet neighborhood was wearisomely long and endlessly depressing. Slashed tires; spray-painted graffiti (including white-supremacist slogans of the ugliest kind);

Unruly teenagers can make life hell in any neighborhood, especially if irresponsible parents make no attempt to control antisocial behavior.

cans full of excrement or urine thrown at passersby; burglaries, acts of vandalism, and verbal assaults—all these and many other charges were laid at the doors of these two households.

There were thefts and burglaries too, and while those responsible were never apprehended, the suspicions of the neighborhood were clear—and surely understandable. The police, the residents said, were reluctant to involve themselves; the Juvenile Probation Department indifferent to their tribulations; both agencies rejected this claim, but it was not hard to see the residents' point of view.

The problem in cases of this kind seems to be that, taken individually, crime for crime, the offenses committed by the teenage troublemakers appear comparatively trivial to the overstretched officers of the various law-enforcement agencies. Taken together in the mass, though—and that is, after all, how the neighbors experience them—they can add up to the tragic destruction of a once happy and peaceful community, like that of Eli Street.

Hiding Behind a False Campaign of Hate

Antagonism between neighbors is common enough for the police to have believed Graham Backhouse's explanation that he was the intended victim of a hate campaign carried out by a neighbor that nearly killed his wife, Margaret. However, the story that unfolded was in fact very different and ended with Backhouse serving life sentences for the murder of a neighbor and the attempted murder of Margaret.

The scarred face of Graham Backhouse. To make it appear that his neighbor had attacked him, he slashed his face and body with a knife. He needed 80 stitches, but it was obvious from the position of the wounds that they were self-inflicted.

How Forensics Exposed the Lie

Backhouse's version was at odds with a great deal of the forensic evidence. His wounds were savage, but it was obvious from their nature that they were self-inflicted. Blood on Bedale-Taylor's hand proved he could not have been holding the knife when he was shot; blood splashes at the scene of the supposed fight were the wrong shape; furniture said to have been knocked over before the shooting had landed on top of bloodstains.

Backhouse's motive was money. The 44-year-old farmer had debts of £70,000 (about $110,000) and decided to murder Margaret for her life insurance money. In the month before the attempt, her coverage had been doubled from £50,000 ($80,000) to £100,000 ($160,000). On April 9, 1984, the couple's Volvo car exploded outside their home, Widdenhall Farm, at Horton, Oxfordshire, when she turned the ignition key. She suffered severe injuries to her buttocks and legs. A bomb, made with piping, shotgun shells, and lead pellets, had been planted in the car and aimed upward through the driver's seat.

Graham Backhouse told the police he had been receiving anonymous letters, and a sheep's head had been impaled on his fence along with a note that read, "You next." He blamed a friend, whom police questioned and let go. Next, he said he suspected his 63-year-old neighbor, Colyn Bedale-Taylor, and he, too, was questioned. Police provided 24-hour protection for Backhouse until he asked them to withdraw it. A panic button, connected to the local police station, was installed instead. Late on April 30, it was activated, and Police Constable Richard Yeadon went into the farmhouse and discovered the body of Colyn Bedale-Taylor, shot in the chest at point-blank range and with a Stanley knife in his hand. In another room, Backhouse lay drenched in blood from deep cuts to his chest and face.

According to Backhouse, Bedale-Taylor had arrived unexpectedly, accused him of being responsible for his son's death in a road accident two years earlier, admitted planting the bomb in the car, and then lashed out with the knife. Backhouse described a struggle, during which he had grabbed his shotgun and fired. However, every piece of evidence at the crime scene pointed to Backhouse luring his neighbor to the farmhouse to kill him so that he could claim the man had admitted to the car bombing and thus lift suspicion of committing that crime from himself.

Margaret Backhouse is interviewed by the press after her discharge from the hospital following the bomb blast. At this point, no one supected that her husband had tried to kill her.

Big hedges are often a source of dispute between neighbors, blocking out light or growing out of control. The law is that land owners may do as they please on their property, provided their actions, such as growing tall trees, do not adversely affect their neighbors' enjoyment.

Trouble with Neighbors

A British Solution

Boundary disputes, which could develop into legal marathons, can now be examined under court-mediation programs in Britain and by similar programs in other countries. Matters are resolved in hours, rather than years. The mediator, usually a lawyer trained in mediation, does not impose a solution, but helps the parties reach their own solution by agreement.

The Curse of the Monster Hedges

An American tree is one of the oddest weapons in a war between neighbors. A chance cross-breeding between two North American species growing in parkland has caused vicious neighbor disputes wherever it is planted and has resulted in changes to laws. Interspecies crossbreeding between the Monterey cypress and the Alaskan cedar produced the Leyland cypress (*Cupressocuparis leylandii*). The Leyland grows up to four feet a year and can reach 100 feet high. It is hardly suitable for a garden hedge, but that is how some home owners have decided to use it.

Michael Jones, 70, victim of his neighbor's hedge in Birmingham, England, set up Hedgeline, which campaigned with some success for legislation against these monster hedges. He had fallen out of favor with his neighbor, Bernard Stanton, 90, when he cut the top off Stanton's hedge as it reached 35 feet high. Legal battles followed, enlivened with accusations of spying, spraying with hoses, and a court appearance for Mr. Stanton's son following a violent encounter. Angry confrontations over these towering hedges have often led to assaults, and one man was shot dead. Usually, the last resort for someone with a difficult neighbor is to move, but that option is denied the owner whose house and garden are in the permanent shadow of a monster hedge. The property is devalued, and sympathetic buyers are difficult to find.

Text-Dependent Questions

1. What can happen when neighbors irritate each other?
2. How dangerous are dogs?
3. What are some sources of disputes between neighbors?

Research Projects

1. How many dog bites occur every year? Who are the main victims? Are certain breeds more likely than others to attack?
2. Pit bulls have a reputation for being especially vicious. Is this merited? Learn about the breed, and find out if they are in fact violent killers or are unfairly maligned.
3. Aside from hedges, what are some other ways neighbors can modify their property to annoy their neighbors and possibly devalue their neighbors' property?

CHAPTER 4

CHILD ABUSE

Words to Understand

Endemic: characteristic of, or prevalent in, a particular field, area, or environment
Hypothermia: subnormal temperature of the body
Pedophile: a person who preys sexually on children
Postpartum: the period of time immediately after the birth of a child
Prelate: a high-ranking church official

CHILD ABUSE IS THE MOST DEPLORABLE CRIME BECAUSE, BY DEFINITION, IT IS INFLICTED BY AN OLDER AND MATURE PERSON ON A SMALLER, PHYSICALLY WEAKER, AND INEXPERIENCED ONE. IT IS ALSO A DESTRUCTIVE CRIME THAT CAN HAVE LONG-LASTING EFFECTS THAT REVERBERATE DOWN THE GENERATIONS. ANYONE WHO WAS BEATEN, INJURED, OR BULLIED DURING THEIR CHILDHOOD STANDS A HIGHER CHANCE OF INFLICTING THE SAME ABUSE ON THEIR OWN CHILDREN.

In the home, children are at risk of several different kinds of abuse. Apart from violent assaults and bullying, they might be subjected to sexual assault by a **pedophile** in the family. Because children have been encouraged over recent years to report abuse, either to support groups or to teachers, the level of recorded crime against them has risen steadily.

Children, especially boys, are often at the greatest risk of being violently abused by their own fathers. Studies in the United States show that a chronically violent man who abuses his wife is also likely to abuse male children in the family.

Breaking the Cycle of Abuse

As societies tackle the problem of child abuse, more and more children are placed on protection registers. In 2013, child protective services agencies across the United States received about 3.5 million referrals involving 6.4 million children. About one-fifth of these children were found to be victims of child abuse and neglect, or about 679,000 children. An estimated 1520 children died from this abuse or neglect. Almost one fourth of victims were children under the age of one. In 60 percent of the homes where a husband beats a wife, the children are abused, too. Children who witness abuse are 50 times more likely to abuse alcohol and drugs, and six times more likely to commit suicide. More than one-third of abused children will repeat the pattern.

False Memory Syndrome

For several years, courts were prepared to convict parents of sexual abuse in cases where the evidence amounted to memories recovered during therapy. Then the growing realization that such memories may not be genuine led to the quashing of some convictions. For the person remembering, there is no difference between a true memory revived during hypnotic regression or some other form of psychological examination and a false one implanted or invented.

In New Jersey, Diane Griggs and her brother, Steve, search the backroads for the sites where their father carried out up to 70 hideous crimes in their presence when they were children. They began to remember during therapy and they remember in intricate detail: bodies in the well, the lake, and the abandoned building; victims tortured, dismembered, burned, or buried. Police searches found nothing. The only proof of their father's guilt is vivid memories, which may not be memories at all.

Research shows that most children from violent homes witness their fathers abusing their mothers. Such terrible experiences can have a destructive effect on the children, causing them to have the same emotional and behavioral problems as children who have been physically abused. Girls may become clinging and withdrawn, while boys often become aggressive.

The Abused Become Abusers

Pedophiles—people who have a sexual appetite for children—frequently leave their victims emotionally damaged. An abused child grows up feeling guilty and unable to form normal sexual relationships, and may in fact become a sexual abuser. Major scandals have brought the issue of pedophilia, and the near impossibility of protecting children, to the forefront. In many countries, men working with children in residential care homes, schools, and clubs have been before the courts.

Around the world, the Roman Catholic Church faces an epidemic of complaints that it has failed to remove guilty priests and has merely tried to avoid scandal by switching them to other parishes, where they have gone on to commit further sex crimes. The Massachusetts office of America's senior **prelate**, Cardinal Bernard Law, supervised the settling of legal actions against some 70 priests at a cost of $10 million in an attempt to keep such outrages hidden. In 2015, the Archdiocese of Milwaukee paid $21 million in an abuse settlement. That year Pope Francis announced that he was setting up a panel to handle allegations of sexual abuse, in an effort to speed up rulings.

A television company exposed a notorious domestic case revolving around a man and his friends who had sexually abused three generations of girls and boys in his family. His children could not persuade the police or social services of his guilt and were left to try and keep their own children safe from him. Inevitably, they failed. One typical aspect of the case was that young children decided to put up with the abuse themselves, hoping it would deflect the grandfather's attention from their brothers and sisters. As is often the case, it turned out that the determined abuser was already violating the other children anyway.

Fred and Rosemary West

When the depravity of Fred and Rosemary West became known, a telling point that emerged was their children's decision to tolerate life at 25 Cromwell Street, Gloucester, in England, rather than risk being separated. Their parents, whom psychiatrists labeled predatory sexual sadists, used their home as a burial ground for the young women victims they brought to the house. Fred West hanged himself before going on trial, and it was Rosemary alone who was convicted on 10 counts of murder and jailed for life. The couple murdered some of their own children and subjected the survivors to beatings, sexual abuse, and rape in what social workers described as the most harrowing of child abuse cases.

Women protest outside the Cathedral of the Holy Cross in Boston where Cardinal Bernard Law was saying Mass. He was later ordered to give evidence in a case brought by 86 victims of the priest John Geoghan.

Fred's rape of his 14-year-old daughter in 1992 led to the full story unfolding. She confided in a friend, whose mother alerted the police. The Wests were charged with rape and cruelty, but the power they exerted was so strong that the children dared not face them across a courtroom. Some retracted their police statements, and the raped girl refused to give evidence. Although the case collapsed, police kept on seeking an older sister, Heather, 16. Initially, they had hoped she would provide additional evidence of rape and sexual abuse, but then they grew concerned that she had disappeared but had not been reported missing. In February 1994, they arrived with a search warrant to look for her body, and within hours, 25 Cromwell Street was infamous as a place where unspeakable crimes had been committed in the midst of what seemed an ordinary family life.

While the Wests' behavior was the most extreme imaginable, and predatory sexual sadists are rare, all child abusers share with them the urge to control and hurt. Paul Britton, a leading psychologist, has stressed that sadistic abusers always choose victims who are old enough to understand what is going to happen to them, because at the heart of sadism is the pleasure that comes from the domination and pain of another.

Brutality to Babies

Up there with apple pie as one of the great, unassailable institutions of American life, motherhood has been held in equal reverence in just about every other culture. Women, the supposed gentler sex, are expected to be at their very gentlest with their own children—and they usually are, which is what makes the occasional exceptions send such a shiver down society's spine.

Behind the facade of normal family life, Fred and Rosemary West descended into the deepest depravity. Psychiatrists argue about which was the dominant partner, and whether suicide was Fred's attempt to shoulder the blame or an act of despair because Rosemary repudiated him.

The case of Susan Smith is a good example: the story of her trial shocked America in 1995, so completely did her conduct appear to have negated her identity as woman and mother. Apparently outraged at her husband's announcement that he was leaving her, Smith drove to a deep lake not far from her home in Union, South Carolina. There, at the top of a steep bank, she got out of her car, released the handbrake and allowed the vehicle to roll down into the water. Her two small sons, sleeping peacefully in the back of the car, were drowned.

When a woman commits a crime as appalling as this, the public tends to be not only distressed but profoundly confused. While the mother's crime seems quite inexplicable in any terms other than those of madness, people fear that an insanity plea will mean the murderer's escaping responsibility.

This was very much the case when Andrea Yates from Houston, Texas, admitted to having drowned her five young children in turn in their bathtub one fateful evening in June 2001. She had killed them, her lawyer acknowledged, and had even done so deliberately—but she should be found not guilty by reason of insanity. In the face of such astonishing behavior, the Texas jury found it could not altogether discount this claim: what else but some profound psychosis could possibly account for a crime so horrific? There was, moreover, much evidence to support the view that Yates was a woman in the grip of some terrible mental illness: she had been hospitalized several times previously for her own safety. In the end, it was decided that her mental state simply had to have some bearing on the crime she had committed: though convicting her of her children's murder, they rejected the prosecutions call for the death penalty.

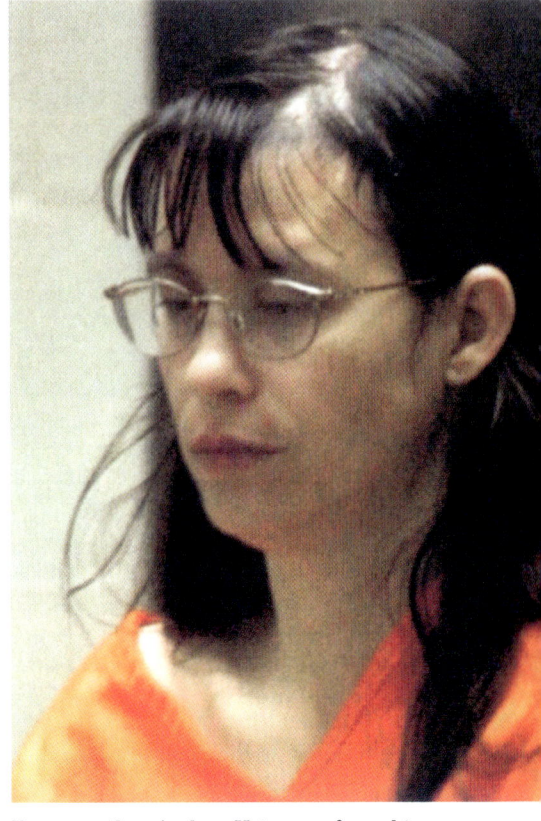

Texas mother Andrea Yates confessed to killing her five children by drowning them in the family bathtub in 2001. At her trial in 2002, she pleaded not guilty by reason of insanity. Despite committing such a terrible crime, her husband supported her plea.

A Children's Memorial Flag

Child abuse is a shameful crime, and it is **endemic** around the globe. Locally and internationally, there are initiatives to make the world a safer place for children. The Child Welfare League of America encourages flying a flag in memory of murdered children during the month of April to keep the youngest victims of violent death in the public mind. Article 19 of the United Nations Children's Rights Charter declares, "Every child should be protected from abuse." There is still some way to go.

Blaming Satan

The death of Victoria Climbie cast light on the plight of African children sent abroad by impoverished parents hoping to give them a better life. Victoria, 8, had traveled from the suburbs of Abidjan, capital of the Ivory Coast, to live with her great aunt, Marie Therese Kouao, first in Paris and then in London. Kouao had offered Berthe and Francis Climbie the opportunity of an education for one of their seven children, and Victoria was selected. Instead, the child was tortured and murdered by Kouao, 45, and her lover, Carl Manning, 28. Kouao had a powerful conviction that Satan was in the little girl and had to be driven out. Victoria was subjected to beatings with a hammer and bicycle chain, scalded, and kept tied in a plastic sack in a bathtub in an unheated room in midwinter. She died of **hypothermia** and 128 injuries to her body. On 12 occasions, doctors, social workers, or the police might have saved her, and so, after Kouao and Manning were jailed for life, a public inquiry was set up to examine why the authorities failed Victoria.

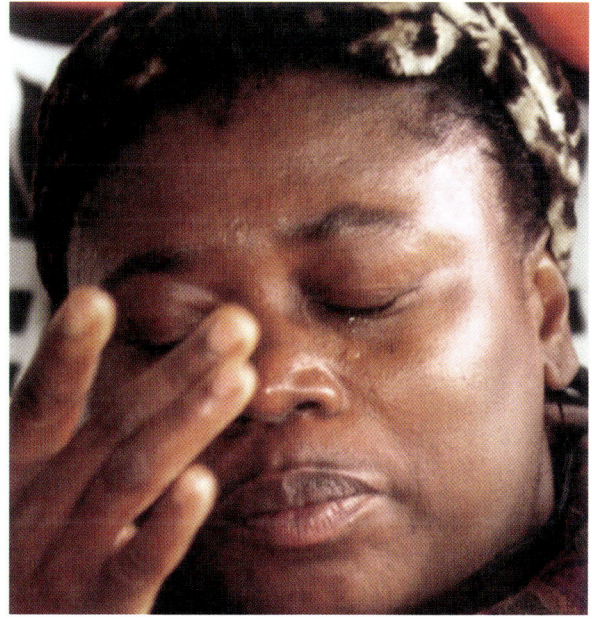

Tearful Berthe Climbie laid flowers and lit candles in London to mark the second anniversary of the death of her daughter Victoria. Like many African parents, the Climbies had entrusted their child to a relative who vowed to care for and educate her.

Infanticide

Different cultures take different attitudes to mothers who kill newborn babies. Infanticide, the proper name for killing an infant, is considered a crime everywhere, but it has long been recognized that the hormonal turmoil of a pregnant woman or mother who has just given birth can cause mental disturbance. At its worst, she may suffer **postpartum** psychosis and harm her baby or herself. Courts in most Western countries would accept she had killed while the balance of her mind was disturbed, and there would be no question of prison. In some states in the United States, however, she would face the death penalty or 15 years in prison.

There are rare cases in which some women appear to have developed a pattern of destroying their offspring. In the United States, for instance, it is believed that two mothers, Marybeth Tinning and Marie Noe, were each responsible for nine baby deaths. However, these are difficult cases for the police and prosecuting lawyers to prove, since it is not always easy to be sure whether babies have died from accidental or deliberate suffocation or whether they succumbed to SIDS (Sudden Infant Death Syndrome), the causes of which are not clear. The actual number of babies who are deliberately killed may never be known.

Text-Dependent Questions

1. How many children are abused each year?
2. What is false memory syndrome?
3. What is a pedophile?

Research Projects

1. What forms can child abuse take? Why are infants so often abused?
2. In the late 20th century, many people were accused of practicing Satanic ritual abuse, a bizarre form of child abuse that turned out to be entirely invented. Investigate this phenomenon. How did it get debunked? How many people were wrongly accused before this happened?
3. Research the Catholic Church child abuse scandal. What happened? What are some explanations for why?

CHAPTER 5

CHILD CRIMINALS

Words to Understand

Bond: the amount of the money guaranteeing that a person released from jail will return to stand trial
Psychopath: a mentally ill or unstable person
Rehabilitation: helping a criminal readapt to society by guidance, retraining, and therapy

CRIMES REFLECT THE SOCIETIES IN WHICH WE LIVE. WHERE THERE IS A DRUG PROBLEM, PEOPLE ARE MUGGED FOR CASH TO FEED THE HABIT. WHEN CAR MANUFACTURERS MAKE IT USELESS TO STEAL A CAR WITHOUT THE IGNITION KEY, OWNERS ARE ATTACKED OR KILLED BECAUSE THE CAR CAN NO LONGER BE STOLEN IN THEIR ABSENCE. WHERE CHILDREN CARRY CELLPHONES, SUPPLIED BY PARENTS ANXIOUS TO GIVE THEM PROTECTION, THEY ARE ROBBED OF THEM. AND THE THIEVES ARE ALMOST CERTAIN TO BE OTHER CHILDREN THEY KNOW, COMMITTING CRIMES TOGETHER IN SMALL GANGS.

Cell phone theft became a modern version of the group lawlessness that some teenagers everywhere have always gone in for, making themselves neighborhood pests until, fortunately, they almost all grow out of it. Yet there is a darker and more dangerous side to criminal behavior among the young. Occasionally, they can kill. When they do, they can commit one of the most tragic of domestic crimes: murdering another child or even a member of their family who cares most for them.

Actresses Melanie Lynskey (left) and Kate Winslet in the film *Heavenly Creatures,* based on the story of teenage friends who killed to avoid being split up. The crime separated them anyway: Pauline Parker and Juliet Hume are held in different prisons and have never met since.

Children Robbing Children

Children robbing children sent national statistics for street crime soaring. In London alone, 3,000 cellular phones were stolen each month during 2001, in spite of the government, police, and telephone providers having formed an anticrime task force. Instead of an improvement, they saw a 73 percent annual rise in thefts of cell phones. Over half the victims were schoolchildren aged 11 to 15. The thieves were most commonly boys aged 14 to 16, although mixed groups and younger children were culprits, too. Cell phone owners of all ages were most vulnerable in the late afternoon, when children left school.

In Westminster, an area in the heart of London, cell phone thefts accounted for nearly half of all street crime. The government argued that telephone companies ought to disable telephones once stolen, but the companies argued that it was ineffective to do so, as well as expensive. While they were arguing, other violent attacks took place: a mugger shot a 19-year-old girl in the head after demanding her cell phone, and a gang robbed 10 children of their cell phones as they left a movie theater. Throughout the U.K., 300,000 cell phone thefts were reported to the police that year, but a Home Office study concluded that the true total of thefts and attempted thefts was nearer 700,000.

Several factors led to the phenomenon. Young criminals had discovered it was an easy way to steal small but costly items to use themselves or to sell. Disabling was ineffective, since criminals had access to cheap software downloads that gave a cell phone a new identity. There was an insatiable demand in Eastern Europe for them, so these high-tech gadgets snatched from children walking home from school were smuggled abroad to be sold to new owners. Most important, stealing cell phones had become a risk-free crime because there were too many cases for the police to investigate more than a fraction of them, and the victim was satisfied by an insurance payout and the chance to upgrade to a better model.

Cell phone theft has only increased since then, though not as a strictly juvenile phenomenon. In 2013, some 3.1 million cell phones were stolen in the United States Phones have become easy to sell; so they are an attractive target for criminals.

Understanding the Concept of Right and Wrong

Each country decides the age of criminal responsibility, the age from which it holds children responsible in the law for their own actions. This hinges on whether a child is mature enough to understand the concept of right and wrong and to behave accordingly. From country to country, and from state to state in the U.S., the age varies.

As society's attitude to children changes, so the age of criminal responsibility can change. For example, in England, it was seven from the Middle Ages until the early 20th century, when it became eight, but in 1963, it was raised to 10 to increase children's rights.

Diverting children away from a life of crime is a priority. Many programs have been tried in the United States, such as training for families with aggressive children, incentives for high school students to graduate, and supervising teenage youths who have been in trouble with the police.

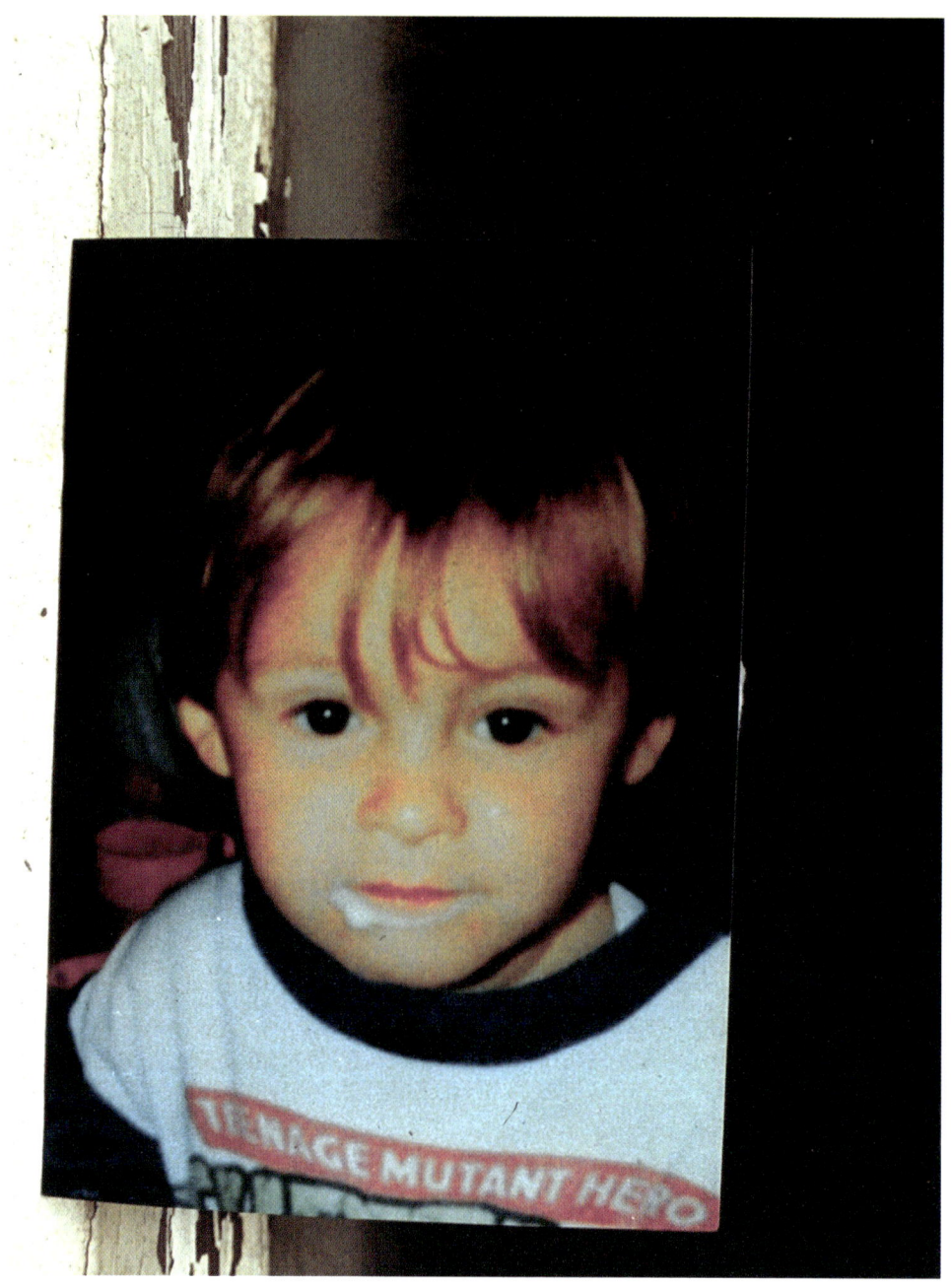

James Bulger, aged two, was led away from his mother while she was shopping, by an older boy. He was then murdered. Video surveillance was used to capture those responsible.

Robert Thompson and Jon Venables were both 10 when they snatched two-year-old James Bulger from a shopping center on Merseyside, in northern England, in the grainy glare of a security camera. The blurred pictures sent a shudder around the world. There they were, two children enticing a baby away from the butcher shop where his mother was shopping, walking hand-in-hand with him, leading him to slaughter. It was powerful evidence that child criminals are prone to act together, and this was an especially heinous crime. After battering James to death, they left his body on a railroad line, where it was run over by a train. The pair were found guilty of killing him and detained in secure units until released on parole after eight years.

Other countries have different approaches to juvenile crime. In Sweden, a boy who murdered another child was not punished by being locked up: the authorities decided that helping the child grow up as a normal member of the community was of more benefit to everyone than labeling him or her a murderer.

A boisterous toddler may strike or shake a baby brother or sister with fatal results, and no one would expect him to have foreseen the consequences of his action. Older children can confuse made-up stories with reality and play lethal games. Two Scandinavian six-year-olds jumped up and down on their five-year-old playmate at school, assuming she would spring up afterward like a cartoon character. Of course, she was dead.

Putting Children in Jail

In Florida in 1999, Lionel Tate, aged 12 and weighing 166 pounds, killed Tiffany Eunick, aged six, and only 46 pounds. He explained they had been wrestling in his living room, copying the moves of professional wrestlers on television. The jury did not believe this because of the extent and severity of Tiffany's injuries. Although his defense team had presented him as an immature boy who could not have realized the outcome of his actions, he was convicted of first-degree murder and sentenced to life in prison without parole. This was one of the harshest punishments to a child in Florida history and reignited the debate about whether child criminals deserved punishment or **rehabilitation**.

When a court decides that a young child is to be detained, there may be a problem. Suitable facilities may not exist, especially if the criminal is a girl. In 1968, Mary Bell, aged 11, an intelligent girl with a pretty, heart-shaped face, was sentenced to life in prison for killing two little boys near her home in Newcastle in the north of England. She had been tried for murder, but found guilty of manslaughter on the grounds of diminished responsibility. Such a sentence would normally have meant she was held in a mental hospital, but, because none would

Lionel Tate (center) is escorted from the courtroom by prison officials after being sentenced to life imprisonment for the murder of six-year-old Tiffany Eunick.

take her, she became the only female in a juvenile detention center until old enough to be transferred to an adult prison. Mary Bell was released in her twenties and went on to lead a normal family life with a daughter of her own.

The Case Of Mary Bell

Her case had begun with the discovery of the body of Martin Brown, four, in an abandoned house. Two days later, the local nursery school was broken into and notes, including one referring to Martin, were left. Then, after two months, Brian Howe, three, was found dead in an area of vacant land, strangled, his body marked with small cuts. During the murder hunt, police suspected the injuries had been inflicted by a child. They questioned 1,200 local children and came upon Mary Bell and her friend, Norma Bell, aged 13. Although they shared the same name, the girls were not related, but were neighbors and close friends.

Eventually, they both went on trial for the two murders. Norma was eventually acquitted. Throughout the proceedings, she was a bewildered child, while the younger Mary appeared self-possessed with an adult's understanding of events. The girls admitted vandalizing a school and leaving notes there, but each blamed the other for the killings. Mary, smart as she was, had made a bad slip. The same day she left the note about Martin Brown, she drew in the class news book a picture of a boy lying beneath a window, exactly the position in which Martin's body had been found. Only someone who had seen it could have known. Chilling details that emerged during the case were that Mary had shown a morbid interest in the children once they were dead.

The Mary Bell case, like that of Venables and Thompson, cast light on the damage family breakdowns and harsh environments cause to children. Sometimes, however, the worst of killers emerges in an ordinary home. Graham Young, a compulsive poisoner, was 14 when he was committed to a hospital for the criminally insane after admitting to murdering his stepmother and attempting to kill his father, sister, and a friend. Released nine years later, he went on to poison work colleagues, killing two of them. After that, he was sent to prison for life.

Misguided Passion

While poisoner Graham Young was a classic example of an uncaring **psychopath**, other young killers were driven by misguided passion. In Saugerties, New York, James Evans, 15, killed his girlfriend's grandmother because Wendy Gardner, the girlfriend, dared him to do it. He is said to have begged Wendy, "If I kill her, will you love me?" And 13-year-old Wendy said yes. The victim was Betty Gardner, 67, who was raising Wendy after her parents split up. Evans strangled her with a

Child Criminals

Mary Bell was only 11 years old when she murdered two young boys. Like the boxer Mike Tyson, commentators point to Mary's traumatic childhood as a possible reason for her behavior–her mother, Betty Bell, ordered nurses to "take that thing away from me" after Mary's birth.

kite string while she was watching television. She had tried to keep the couple apart because of Evans' reputation for violence.

Wendy and James were both sentenced to life imprisonment. During the killing and for three days after it, Wendy had held her young sister prisoner. When the girl finally escaped, the story came out: murder, a spending spree with the victim's money, and failed attempts to dispose of Betty Gardner's body, which was still in the trunk of her car.

The relationship that drove Pauline Parker, 16, and Juliet Hume, 15, to kill Pauline's mother was no less intense. They feared being split up because the Humes were planning to leave New Zealand. Pauline was determined to follow them to South Africa, but knew her mother would stand in her way. The pair killed her by smashing her head with a brick in a stocking while they were all out walking. Then they pretended to have found her dead. Their claim that she had died by falling and hitting her head was never believed because she had 45 injuries. The pair were found guilty of murder. Because of their ages, they were sentenced "to be detained during Her Majesty's Pleasure."

After their release, Juliet Hume moved to Britain. She lives in Scotland and writes crime fiction under the pseudonym Anne Perry. Interest in her own story was revived with the success of the film *Heavenly Creatures,* based on the murder of Mrs. Honora Mary Parker. The film, starring Kate Winslet and Melanie Lynskey as Hume and Parker, made clear the lesbian overtones, which had troubled the girls' families and added notoriety to the case when they were on trial in 1954.

"The Reason Being a Desire to Kill."

A child tried for murder is extremely rare. Perhaps Harold Jones is the only one who faced two trials as a child for killing other children. He was 15, the year was 1921. In the first case, he was found not guilty of killing Freda Burnell, eight, who disappeared while on an errand to the seed shop where he worked, close to her home in Abertillery, Wales. The next day, her body was found nearby. Freda had died of shock and partial strangulation, and there had been an attempt at rape. When her handkerchief was discovered in a shed behind the shop, Jones was arrested. His acquittal brought cheers because few believed the young shop assistant could have done it.

But two weeks later, the body of Florence Little, 11, was found in the attic of Harold Jones's home. This time he confessed, saying he had cut her throat with a kitchen knife and sexually assaulted her, "The reason being a desire to kill." At the second trial, he pleaded guilty to murdering Florence Little and was sentenced to be "detained at His Majesty's Pleasure." He then confessed that he had indeed been guilty of murdering young Freda Burnell.

Fearful of being split up, Juliet Hume (above) and Pauline Parker murdered Pauline's mother in a classic example of misguided teenage reasoning. Both girls were actually very intelligent, writing film scripts, novels, and creating a medieval fantasy world for their stories called Borovnia.

The Case of Constance Kent

A 16-year-old girl who got away with murder was Constance Kent. Victorian England was intrigued by the mysterious death of her half-brother, Francis, at the age of four. The boy was taken from his crib at the family home in Road, Wiltshire, and dumped in the outside toilet with his throat horribly slit. The parents, six children, and three servants were in the house that night, but no one had heard anything alarming. There were no signs of a forced entry, so the police suspected the killer was a member of the household, although they could not detect any obvious motive. They lost their only clue, a bloodstained nightdress, found in the boiler flue. Although there was no evidence who it belonged to, Constance was arrested and charged with murder, only to be released on her father's **bond**. Months later, the children's nurse was arrested but released without charge, and the murder became a famous mystery.

Until, that is, Constance Kent confessed. For five years, she kept the secret that she had killed Francis because she felt replaced in her father's affections. However, sent to live at a convent in France because she had a bad relationship with her stepmother, she acquired a deep religious faith. She decided to sail back to England and confess to the crime. Constance Kent was tried in 1865, pleaded guilty to murder, and was sentenced to death. This was later changed to life imprisonment, and she served 20 years for killing her baby half-brother. She died in 1944.

The essence of her story—a black deed at the heart of a respectable family and the tormented mind of the undetected killer—continues to appeal to crime writers. Francis King's novel *Act of Darkness* mirrors the murder mystery and relationships of the Constance Kent story, although he moved his tale into the 20th century and gave it a more exotic location than England.

School Shootings

In the last 10 years, more than 40 children have been killed in school shootings across the United States, mostly by fellow (or former) pupils. The most deadly cases include Columbine High School, in Littleton, Colorado, where 14 students and one teacher were killed by two teenage boys in 1999; the killing of four students and one teacher at the Westside Middle School, in Jonesboro, Arkansas, where two boys shot at their classmates from a nearby woods after a false fire alarm; and Santana High School, San Diego (pictured), where a

15-year-old boy killed two fellow students and injured 13 others in 2001. In the infamous Sandy Hook case, 20-year-old Adam Lanza took a gun to the school where his mother taught and shot her, six adults, and 20 first-grade students.

Why would children want to shoot their classmates? Investigations of school shootings since 1974 found that students who came to school with a plan to kill did not just "snap." They warned classmates, aired their grievances, and left other clues. In many cases, the attackers said they felt persecuted or bullied. Many either threatened to commit suicide or actually tried it.

Researchers have warned against profiling students, saying there is no common profile of a school shooter (although in all cases they have been boys). Rather than building a profile of an attacker with a set of personality traits, schools should focus on behavior and encourage students to speak out about students who are threatening violence.

Text-Dependent Questions

1. What is the age of criminal responsibility?
2. How old were Jon Venables and Robert Thompson when they committed their crime? How old was their victim, James Bulger?
3. What is the difference between punishment and rehabilitation?

Research Projects

1. How prevalent is juvenile crime in your state? What crimes are the most common?
2. How should juvenile criminals be handled? Should children and teenagers be tried and convicted as if they were adults?
3. Choose a famous example of a juvenile criminal. Find out what made him or her decide to commit a serious crime, and what happened afterward.

CHAPTER 6

LIFE AFTER CRIME

Words to Understand

Domestic: related to home and family
Sentence: a punishment issued to a convicted criminal
Torture: inflicting severe pain as a punishment or as a means of coercion

COMMITTING A **domestic** CRIME MIGHT TAKE ONLY MINUTES, BUT THE AFTEREFFECTS CAN LAST A LIFETIME. RELATIONSHIPS ARE FOREVER ALTERED. FAMILY LIFE MIGHT BE COMPLETELY DESTROYED. AND UNLIKE CRIMES THAT INVOLVE STRANGERS, A DOMESTIC CRIME IS UP CLOSE AND PERSONAL. IT STAYS THAT WAY, AND THERE IS NO TIME LIMIT ON REGRET.

Usually, the bad things that people do in their youth trouble them more in later life. If it was a crime, the burden can lie heavily. A prison **sentence** may have been served, a fine may have been paid, but the matter is not so readily expunged from the conscience. From time to time, a killer may confess to a crime committed many years in the past. Sometimes, this is because of the risk of a cold case being reopened with new techniques, such as DNA testing, leading to him being identified as the culprit after all. For others, there is an undeniable

The consequences of committing crime are usually far-reaching and can last a lifetime. The cycle of prison, release, and reoffending is a common one. In the West, up to 75 percent of prisoners will have reoffended within two years of release from prison.

urge to unburden the guilt, the same reason that drove Constance Kent to own up and lift the shadow of suspicion from the rest of the household. She knew the death penalty must be passed and she could not rely on it being commuted to a life sentence, as it was.

Paying the Price for Committing Crime

Depending on the severity of the crime and which state it is committed in, a wrong-doer in the United States may be sentenced to punishments ranging from execution or incarceration in a super-jail, at one end of the spectrum, to home custody, fines, or community service at the other. European countries, along with many others, no longer have the death penalty. It remains on the statute book in the U.K. as a penalty for treason, although no one has been executed there since the 1950s.

The way in which a society handles its criminals depends on how far it is committed to rehabilitation or whether it seeks purely to punish. Another factor is expense, because even a society that claims to prefer rehabilitation may not provide it if insufficient funds are available. In the U.K., which locks up a higher proportion of its population than other comparable European countries, the argument never goes away. Prison removes offenders for a while, but without education and efforts to help them repair their lives and create a more secure future, it returns them to society having learned only how to lead a life of crime.

Among the world's toughest prison regimes are the U.S. "supermax jails," as maximum-security jails are popularly known. Toward the end of the last century, more than 50 were built to house felons too violent for other prisons. Within 20 years, they held 20,000 inmates. Because there were not enough violent psychopaths, other categories were used to fill them up, usually the mentally ill and ethnic minorities. Prisoners are held in solitary confinement 23 hours a day in sealed metal cells where lights are never turned off and any contact with other prisoners is impossible. One hour is allowed for exercise and it is spent alone in a bare room. Human Rights Watch has objected that such conditions violate the United Nations international covenant on civil and political rights and the convention against **torture**. By 2015, a number of jurisdictions were beginning to seriously question the value of solitary confinement.

Efforts at Rehabilitation

While supermax jails capture headlines, the rehabilitation efforts of the Office of Justice's Re-entry of Offenders Programs, which affect the majority of prisoners, proceed without fanfare. Law enforcement agencies, social services, victim support groups, and neighborhood organizations are all involved in this work. Each federal prison has services to help inmates become useful members of society. Treatment is available for substance abuse and mental health problems. Furlough—a period of temporary release—helps prisoners maintain family ties and is useful during the transitional period before a sentence ends. Inmate placement programs help prisoners find employment on their release from jail by preparing them for job interviews. Parenting programs teach them to cope with the ill effects their imprisonment will have had on their families. Many learn the literacy skills they failed to grasp while at school.

Fighting youth crime is high on the agendas in all developed countries, which have seen a sharp rise in teenage-related incidents in the last 40 years. Boot camps, like this one, administer a "short, sharp shock" of military-style discipline to young offenders.

A boot camp inmate holds up his ID card. The effectiveness of these military-style camps in preventing reoffending is under question. The boot camps that provide no facilities for education or rehabilitation are the ones with the highest reoffending rates.

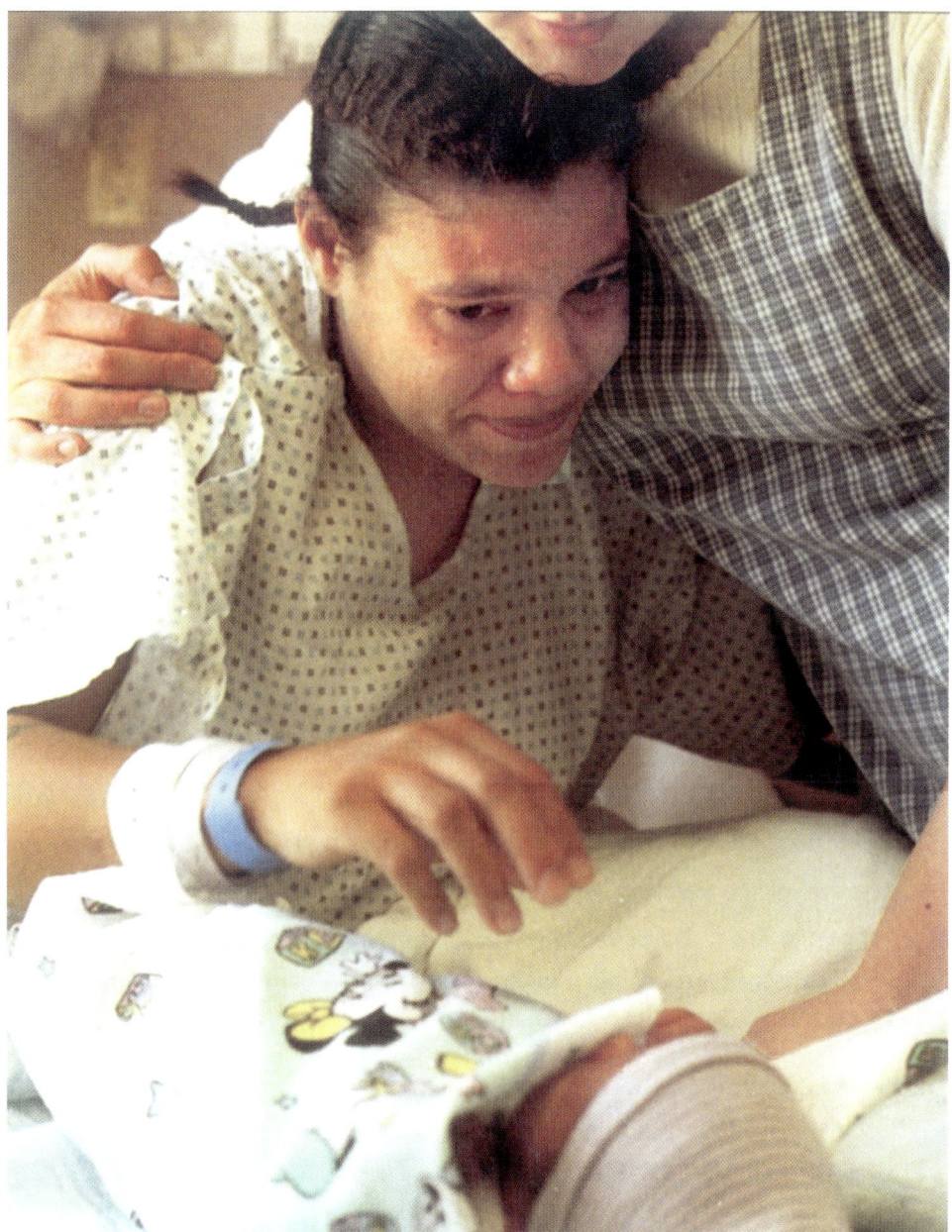

As well as the personal effects of crime, the impact on families can be devastating. Here a mother must put her newborn child into temporary care while she finishes her prison sentence.

Life After Crime

Young criminals held in young-offender institutions are particularly encouraged to improve their education as a way of reducing the likelihood that they will reoffend. Some qualify for university entrance before they are freed, while others acquire practical skills that will make it easier to hold down a job. Work training may take place during the sentence or be available afterward, all aimed at providing a future away from crime.

Theories are admirable; practice often fails. Overcrowded young-offender institutions result in youngsters being sent to adult prisons, where the special programs aimed at rehabilitation for their age group are out of reach. The focus on Florida, after it sentenced Lionel Tate to life without parole for a crime committed when he was 12, revealed that in its determination to curb crime among the young, the state was sending a quarter of its juvenile inmates to adult prisons. One in 13 of its prison population was serving time for a crime committed as a juvenile.

Criminologists have long accepted that younger offenders are more likely to reoffend than older ones, and a Department of Corrections study of the situation in Florida confirmed it: they reoffend at higher rates and they do it sooner after release. For the period between 2004 and 2011, those who committed a crime under the age of 25 had a 34 percent chance of committing another crime shortly after release. Among criminals aged 35 to 49 at their first offence, the rate of recidivism was only 16 percent. The younger an inmate at the time of a first offense, the more likely he or she is to commit future crimes that will result in a return to prison.

I Was Abused, So I Abuse

It is also consistent for people before the courts for crimes of violence or abuse to claim they had themselves been childhood victims of abuse. This makes it appear inevitable that mistreated children will become the next generation of abusers. However, it is worth stressing that the majority do not repeat the pattern. The U.S. Department of Health and Human Services has reported that one-third copy the torment inflicted on them.

The figure is bad enough, but it does demonstrate that two-thirds do not do so. Having been a victim is not enough to explain, let alone excuse, the behavior of the violent or abusive adult.

Everyone working with damaged children or violent adults agrees it is imperative to break the cycle—the problem is how to do it and make it stick. People will have committed crimes before they are offered advice about anger management or the chance to explore reasons for their behavior and ways of improving their responses to other people. Therefore, the results of the Canadian program that focused on teenagers (described in Chapter Four) were especially encouraging.

Through the STOP (Services, Training, Officers, and Prosecutors) Violence Against Women program, the United States Department of Justice offers grants to states to provide support and services to women who have suffered domestic violence or been abused in some other way. Help is also provided through the National Domestic Violence Hotline, where dedicated staff can offer help and advice and respond to emergencies 24 hours a day.

Family and friends of the murdered two-year-old, James Bulger, campaign in England against the release on parole of one of his killers, Jon Venables, who was 10 when he committed this crime. His release in 2001 ignited the debate about retribution and rehabilitation in the justice system.

Usually, subjects for study are male prisoners. One consultant psychiatrist to an English prison, Bob Jones, who worked with more than 50 murderers, came to the conclusion that, "Child murderers are uncommon, but lethal infantile rage is commonplace." He described the men as emotionally stunted by the violence they had suffered themselves as children and said that their own outbursts of violence that landed them in prison were the equivalent of childish tantrums. Accepting his theory, the prisoners recognized when their behavior was immature and they learned to amend it to be more adult and civilized.

Venables and Thompson

You will never meet Jon Venables or Robert Thompson. Those names vanished during the rehabilitation of the boys who enticed two-year-old James Bulger from his mother's side and murdered him. Eight years after their trial, the killers were released, but with new identities to safeguard them from publicity, particularly because of death threats from the Bulger family and its friends. As the perpetrators of such an infamous crime, they have no hope of normal lives unless their real identities are kept secret. There was disquiet when, aged 10, they were tried in an adult court. Then, the eight years the judge recommended that they be incarcerated was increased to 15 by the Home Secretary, a decision reversed after a legal battle.

The boys were held in separate secure units. The U.K. has 28 units providing 300 places and offering intensive rehabilitation programs to child rapists, arsonists, and murderers. The regime is strict, but standards of education and therapy are high, and there are long periods of useful activity. There are no bars, no shared cells, and low numbers of inmates. The system is based on incentives, allowing well-behaved children who show self-control and an awareness of the consequences of their actions to earn rewards. From a cell with only a bed, they can progress to a room with television and books. Rather than cut them off from the outside world, visits to pubs, soccer games, and shopping centers keep them in touch.

By summer 2001, a decision had to be taken about the future of Thompson and Venables. At 18, they would be too old for a secure unit. The choice was between releasing them or transferring them to a young-offender unit within the prison system. The parole board decided on release after lengthy interviews with each boy and written statements from them, in addition to reports from their secure units, probation officers, and psychological profiles. The board needed to be satisfied about their remorse for the crime. Because Jon Venables had cried throughout the trial and apologized to James Bulger's mother, his remorse was never in doubt. But Robert Thompson, regarded as the dominant character, had not accepted responsibility for the crime until 1999.

Rehabilitation or Retribution?

When he committed the murder, Thompson was barely literate, bullied by older brothers, and habitually skipped school. By contrast, he left the secure unit having passed school exams and with a strong interest in design and fashion. Jon Venables had developed into an avid soccer fan and was expected to go to university.

Like all released murderers, they were freed on parole, that is, they could be returned to prison at any time if their behavior ever gives cause for concern. From the secure unit, they would have been moved to hostels or safe houses where counseling and supervision is provided to ease serious criminals back into society. When they move on, they must report every change of address, any further education, and every relationship to their probation officer.

After five years, their lawyers could ask for this reporting restriction to be lifted, but it is likely to remain in the case of Thompson and Venables. Two clerks at the Parole Life License Unit at the Home Office monitor their probation officers' concerns for the rest of their lives. Previous experience of releasing children who have been rehabilitated at secure units shows they do not kill again, but in trying to live with what they have done, they may turn to alcohol and drugs and risk mental illness in the future. In 2010 John Venables was jailed again for possessing child pornography. He was freed in 2013 and given a false identify, his fourth since the murder.

The release of Thompson and Venables angered pressure groups, such as Mothers Against Murder and Aggression, and Justice for James, who had campaigned for them to be moved into the prison system. The controversy highlighted opposing attitudes to criminals: retribution versus rehabilitation. By sending the pair to secure units, the authorities were determined to make a rigorous effort at rehabilitation. In releasing them, they demonstrated they had succeeded in this aim. A powerful argument in favor of releasing the pair, or any 18-year-old in the same position, was that the young-offender institutions are prisons where life is brutal, and where the expensive and careful nurturing of years in a secure unit is guaranteed to be undone.

Relinquishing the Rage of Revenge

When the families of victims of the Oklahoma City bombing were told they could watch Timothy McVeigh (pictured) die on closed circuit television, many, like Dan McKinney, who lost his wife, and Diane Marino, who lost her son, were overjoyed.

However, Bud Welch, whose daughter Julie was killed, had discovered by then that he needed to heal himself rather than waste emotion on her killer. Explaining why he had changed his mind about wanting McVeigh dead, he said he was tired of the pain he was inflicting on himself by hoping for an act of "revenge and rage." Relinquishing the quest had given him release, he said.

Lesley Moreland, whose daughter Ruth was stabbed to death, described her own journey from revenge to reconciliation in *An Ordinary Murder*. She visited Ruth's killer in prison and found him remorseful. Then she corresponded with a murderer on Death Row and "learned that a killer is more than his evil deed."

Dealing with the Loss

Marian Partington has written movingly about the loss of her younger sister Lucy, who died at the hands of Fred and Rosemary West. During the 20 years that Lucy was missing, her family, like the families of all missing people, suffered the ache of unresolved loss. Her cousin, the novelist Martin Amis, has described how, unconsciously, he let a missing girl become a thread running through his novels.

With the discoveries at 25 Cromwell Street came certainty that, in Marian's words, "Lucy had suffered a death beyond our worst imaginings." Learning to live with the pain, Marian Partington uses these words from the Dalai Lama, which offer a way to break the cycle of violence and hatred.

"I will learn to cherish beings of bad nature And those pressed by strong sins and suffering As if I had found a precious Treasure very difficult to find."

The teenage son of a murdered father delivers a victim impact statement about the effect the crime has had on him. Bringing criminal and victim face-to-face outside the courtroom is also used as a direct method of showing the offender the terrible impact his crime has had.

The Grief of the Victims

In recent years, the effects of serious crimes on victims' families have been studied, too. It was found that their grieving was stalled during the judicial process, and they also suffered from feeling left out. As a result, attempts are made to involve them more. In the United States, they can now meet the killer. They can make statements in court about the impact of the crime on their lives. In Texas and a dozen other states, they can watch the killer die. However, as research by social commentators, such as Angela Neustatter, revealed, their euphoria at an execution is brief, and rather than lead to closure, the full force of delayed grief overwhelms them.

Text-Dependent Questions

1. Where do people end up after they are convicted of crimes?
2. How do prisons attempt to rehabilitate prisoners?
3. How likely is an abused child to become a criminal?

Research Projects

1. What are some steps criminal justice organizations take to reduce recidivism?
2. Should victims and/or their families have any say in what happens to the criminals who have harmed them? Why or why not?
3. Is it possible to teach an abused child healthier ways of interacting with people? Research programs that aim to stop the cycle of abuse and crime.

SERIES GLOSSARY

Amnesty: pardon given by a country to citizens who have committed crimes

Anarchist: a person who wants to do away with organized society and government

Antiglobalization: against large companies or economies spreading into other nations

Appeal: referral of a case to a higher court for review

Arraignment: a formal court hearing at which the prisoner is asked whether he or she pleads "guilty" or "not guilty" to the charge or charges

Bifurcated: divided into two branches or parts

Bioassay: chemical analysis of biological samples

Biometrics: use of physical characteristics, such as fingerprints and voice, to identify users

Certificate of certiorari: a document that a losing party files with the Supreme Court, asking the Supreme Court to review the decision of a lower court; it includes a list of the parties, a statement of the facts of the case, and arguments as to why the court should grant the writ

Circumstantial evidence: evidence that can contribute to the conviction of an accused person but that is not considered sufficient without eyewitness or forensic evidence

Civil disobedience: refusing, in a peaceful way, to obey a government policy or law

Clemency: an act of leniency or mercy, especially to moderate the severity of punishment due

Commute: to change a penalty to another one less severe

Cryptology: the science and art of making and breaking codes and ciphers

Dactylography: the original name for the taking and analysis of fingerprints

Deputy: a person appointed as a substitute with power to act

Dissident: someone who disagrees with an established religious or political system, organization, or belief

Distributed Denial of Service (DDOS) attack: a malware attack that floods all the bandwidth of a system or server, causing the system to be unable to service real business

Effigy: a model or dummy of someone

Electronic tagging: the attaching of an electronic device to a criminal after he or she has been released, in order to track the person to ensure that he or she does not commit a crime again

Ethics: the discipline dealing with what is good and bad and with moral duty and obligation

Euthanasia: the act of killing or permitting the death of hopelessly sick or injured individuals in a relatively painless way for reasons of mercy

Exhume: to dig up a corpse, usually for examination

Exoneration: a finding that a person is not in fact guilty of the crime for which he or she has been accused

Extortion: the act of obtaining money from a person by force, intimidation, or undue or illegal power

Forensics: the scientific analysis and review of the physical and medical evidence of a crime

Garrote: to strangle someone using a thin wire with handles at either end

Gibbet: an upright post with a projecting arm for hanging the bodies of executed criminals as a warning

Graft: the acquisition of gain (as money) in dishonest or questionable ways

Grievance: a real or imagined wrong, for which there are thought to be reasonable grounds for complaint

Heresy: religious convictions contrary to church dogma and that deviate from orthodox belief

Hulk: a ship used as a prison

Hypostasis: the migration of blood to the lowest parts of a dead body, caused by the effect of gravity

Incendiary: a bomb

Infiltrate: to enter or become established in gradually or unobtrusively, usually for subversive purposes

Intern (v.): to confine or impound, especially during a war

Interpol: an association of national police forces that promotes cooperation and mutual assistance in apprehending international criminals and criminals who flee abroad to avoid justice

Intrusion detection system (IDS): software designed to detect misuse of a system

Junta: a group of military officers who hold power, usually as the result of a coup

Jurisprudence: a system or body of law

Ladder: an early form of the rack in which the victim was tied to a vertical framework and weights were attached to his ankles

Lag: a convict

Latent: present and capable of becoming obvious, or active, even though not currently visible

Lockstep: a mode of marching in step where people move one after another as closely as possible

Lynch: to attack and kill a person, typically by hanging, without involvement of the courts or legal system and often done by a mob

Manifesto: a written statement declaring publicly the intentions, motives, or views of its issuer

Manslaughter: the unlawful killing of a human being without express or implied intent

Martyrdom: the suffering of death on account of adherence to a cause and especially to one's religious faith

Mercenary: a man or woman who is paid by a foreign government or organization to fight in its service

Miscreant: one who behaves criminally or viciously

Molotov cocktail: an explosive weapon; each "cocktail" is a bottle filled with gasoline and wrapped in a rag or plugged with a wick, then ignited and thrown

Money laundering: to transfer illegally obtained money through an outside party to conceal the true source

Mule: a person who smuggles drugs inside his or her body

Mutinous: to resist lawful authority

Paramilitary: of, relating to, being, or characteristic of a force formed on a military pattern, especially as a potential auxiliary military force

Pathologist: a physician who specializes in examining tissue samples and fluids to diagnose diseases

PCR: polymerase chain reaction, a technique of making multiple copies of a small section of DNA so that it can be analyzed and identified

Personal alarm: a small electronic device that a person can carry and activate if he or she feels threatened

Phreaker: a person who hacks telephone systems

Pillory: a device formerly used for publicly punishing offenders consisting of a wooden frame with holes in which the head and hands can be locked

Political asylum: permitting foreigners to settle in your country to escape danger in another country, usually his or her native land

Postmortem: an autopsy; an examination of a dead body, looking for causes of death

Precedent: something done or said that serves as an example or rule to authorize or justify a subsequent act of similar kind

Pyramid scheme: an investment swindle in which some early investors are paid off with money put up by later ones in order to encourage more and bigger risks; also called a Ponzi scheme

Quick: the living flesh beneath the fingernails

Racketeering: the act of conducting a fraudulent scheme or activity

Ratchet: a mechanism consisting of a "pawl," a hinged catch that slips into sloping teeth of a cogwheel, so that it can be turned only in one direction

Repatriation: returning a person to his or her country of origin

Ruse: a subterfuge in order to distract someone's attention

Screw: slang term for a prison guard

Scuttle: to cut a hole through the bottom, deck, or side of a ship

Seditious: of, relating to, or tending toward an incitement of resistance to or insurrection against lawful authority

Serology: the laboratory analysis of blood serum, particularly in the detection of blood groups and antibodies

Siege (n.): a standoff situation, in which a group holds a position by force and refuses to surrender

Slander: a false and defamatory oral statement about a person

Smash and grab: a term used to describe a method of stealing, where thieves break windows (for example, on a shop front or a car) to grab the goods within before fleeing

Statute: a law enacted by the legislative branch of a government

Statutory: authorized by the statute that defines the law

Subversive: characterized by systematic attempts to overthrow or undermine a government or political system by persons working secretly from within

Succinylcholine: a synthetic drug that paralyzes muscle fiber

Vendetta: an often-prolonged series of retaliatory, vengeful, or hostile acts or exchange of such acts

White-collar crime: crime committed by office staff, usually involving theft from the company they work for

Worm: a computer program that enters one computer and replicates itself to spread to other computers; unlike a virus, it does not have to attach itself to other files

Xenophobic: having an unreasonable fear of what is foreign and especially of people of foreign origin

CHRONOLOGY

Prehistory: Biblical story of sibling rivalry: Cain and Abel.

1868: Constance Kent tried for her brother's murder.

1921: Harold Jones tried twice for murdering different girls

1954: Pauline Parker and Juliet Hume kill Honora Parker

1955: Ruth Ellis becomes last woman to be executed in the U.K

1968: Mary Bell found guilty of manslaughter

1971–99: *Jones v. Stanton leylandii* hedge dispute.

1972: Graham Young found guilty of poisoning.

1980s: United States begins building supermax prisons.

1980: Jean Harris shoots Dr. Herman Tarntower.

1981–99: *Powling v Woolls* garden boundary dispute.

1984: Graham Backhouse murders his neighbor and attempts to kill his wife

1988–99: *Insley v. Wibberley* garden boundary dispute.

1990: Sara Thornton is convicted of murder.

1992: Mike Tyson is convicted of raping a Miss Black America contestant.

1993: James Bulger killed by Robert Thompson and Jon Venables in Liverpool, England.

1994: Fred and Rosemary West, serial killers and abusers, unmasked; James Evans and Wendy Gardner kill her grandmother.

1994: Violence Against Women Act passed; annual rates of domestic violence subsequently drop 64 percent by 2013.

1995: Violence Against Women Office of the U.S. Office of Justice Programs created O.J. Simpson accused of murder of exwife and partner; Susan Smith convicted of murdering her two sons in South Carolina.

1997: Sheila Bellush becomes a victim of killers hired by her ex-husband.

1999: Julie Scully murdered in Greece by her lover; Lionel Tate murders Tiffany Eunick.

2000: Anthony Hurdle, serial stalker, convicted of attempted murder; Andrew Cromar fined for annoying neighbors with garden ornaments; Victoria Climbie tortured and murdered by Kuoao and Manning; child protection rules tightened following death of Lauren Wright.

2001: Anne Heche publishes *Call Me Crazy* about her own recovered memory; Jane Andrews kills Thomas Cressman; Crown Prince Dipendra of Nepal shoots royal family; Elaine Meredith damages neighbors' cars; Dorothy Evans convicted of harassing neighbors; Diane Whipple killed by neighbors' Presa Canario dogs; Sarah Bland satanic abuse case debated in Northern Ireland Assembly.

2002: Cardinal Bernard Law under attack for protecting pedophile priests; in Texas, Andrea Yates convicted of murdering her five children by drowning them in the bath.

2012: Adam Lanza shoots 28 people at Sandy Hook Elementary School in Newtown, Connecticut.

2014: Vatican reveals details of how it handled the priests who committed child abuse.

FURTHER INFORMATION

Useful Web Sites

Child Welfare League of America: www.cwla.org/advocacy/memorialflag.htm

Children's Bureau: www.acf.hhs.gov

Crime in the United States: https://www2.fbi.gov/ucr/cius2009/index.html

Office on Violence Against Women: http://www.justice.gov/ovw

Further Reading

David, Ann. *Women Who Kill.* Boston: Beacon Press, 1996.

DeFelice, Jim. *Kill Grandma For Me.* New York: Kensington Pub., 1998.

Gaute, J.H.H. and O'Dell, Robin. *The New Murderers' Who's Who.* New York: International Polygonics, 1991.

Herman, Judith. *Trauma and Recovery: The Aftermath of Violence from Domestic Abuse to Political Terror.* New York: Basic Books, 2015.

Glatt, John. *Blind Passion.* New York: St. Martin's Press, 2000.

Jukes, Adam. *Why Men Hate Women.* London: Free Association Books, 1993.

Leonard, Elizabeth D. *Convicted Survivors: The Imprisonment of Battered Women Who Kill.* New York: State University of New York Press, 2002.

Parker, Tony. *Life After Life: Interviews with Twelve Murderers.* London: Seeker & Warburg, 1990.

Scott, Alexander. *Parents Who Kill.* Amazon Digital Services, 2015.

Weiss, Elain and Michael Magill. *Surviving Domestic Violence: Voices of Women Who Broke Free. Salt* Lake City, UT: Agreka, 2000.

About the Author

Isobel Brown has been writing about crime for most of her career. As a young newspaper court reporter, she became fascinated by its effects on both criminals and victims. Those years, she says, were an unwitting apprenticeship for her later work as a novelist.

In the years between the crime reporting and the novel writing, she was a feature writer on *The Guardian* in London, England. She has worked as a writer in residence in prisons and young offender institutions, as well as at universities and creative writing centers in England and other European countries. Her own writing has been shortlisted for literary prizes, although, as she says, she has never won anything in her life. She is currently a writing fellow at Cambridge University. She is married and lives in London.

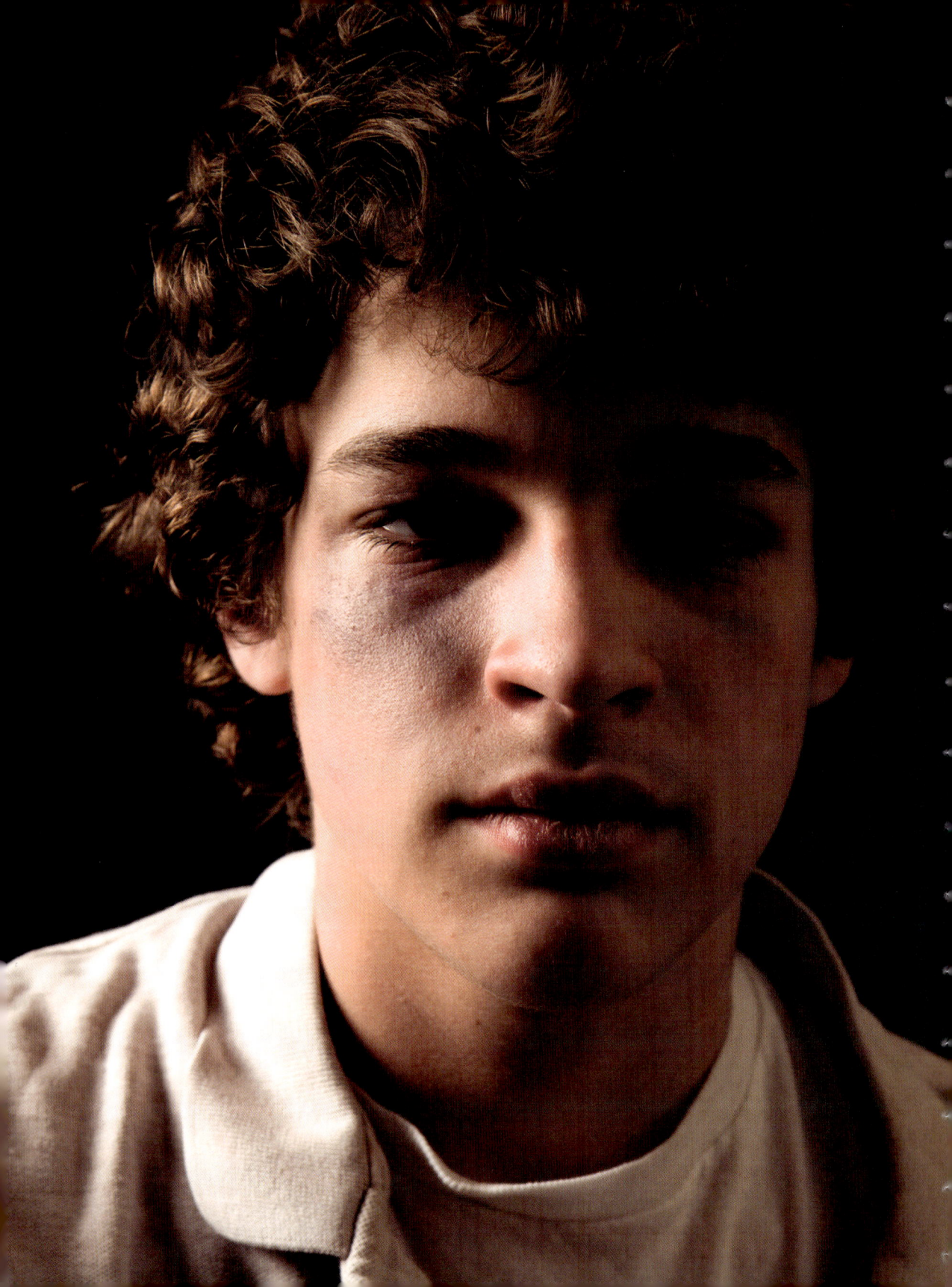

INDEX

Act of Darkness 65
abuse 8, 11, 13, 21–22, 24, 26, 30, 34, 45–47, 49, 51, 71, 74–75, 89–91
   breaking cycle of 46
   domestic 22, 24, 26, 91
   effects of 45
   physical 11–13, 18, 22–23, 30, 34, 46
   substance 71
   verbal 34
Amis, Martin 80
Andrews, Jane 17–19, 90
anger-management programs 24
Atwood, Margaret 22

babies 27, 49, 52
   brutality to 49–50
   infanticide 52
Backhouse, Graham 38–39, 89
Backhouse, Margaret 38–40
Bedale-Taylor, Colyn 39
Bell, Mary 59, 61–62, 89
Bellush, Sheila 26–28, 90
Blackthorne, Allen 26–28
Blakely, David 13–15, 18
Bland, Sarah 90
Bobbit, Lorena 13
boot camps 70–72
boundary disputes 42, 89
Britton, Paul 49
Brown, Martin 61
Brown, Nicole 24
Bulger, James 58–59, 89
Burnell, Freda 63
Burstow, Anthony 25–26

children 17, 21, 24, 35–36, 45–47, 49–51, 55–61, 63, 65–66, 74, 76–78, 90–91
   abuse 21, 25, 45–53
   breaking cycle of 46
   effects of 45
criminals 55–56, 59, 70, 74, 79, 84–85
   family breakdown and 61, 69, 71
   imprisonment 25, 27–28, 60, 63, 65, 91

sexual assaults on 18, 24, 45, 63
witnessing abuse 46
Climbié, Victoria 51, 90
conscience 69
Cressman, Thomas 17–19, 90
criminal responsibility, age of 56–57
Cromar, Andrew 34, 90

Dance With a Stranger 15
Del Toro, Jose Luis 28
Dipendra, Crown Prince 21, 23, 90

Ellis, Ruth 13–15, 18, 89
Embry, Teresa 36
Eunick, Tiffany 59–60, 90
Evans, James 61–63, 89

false memory syndrome 46

Gardner, Wendy 61–63, 89
Geoghan, John 48
Givens, Robin 24
Goldman, Ronald 24
Griggs, Diane 46

Harris, Jean 16, 18, 89
hate campaign 38–39
Heavenly Creatures 55, 63
Heche, Anne 90
hedges 41–42
Howe, Brian 61
Hume, Juliet 55, 63–64, 89
Hurdle, Anthony 25–26, 90

infanticide 52
insanity 50

Johnson, John 25
Jones, Bob 76
Jones, Harold 63, 89
Jones, Michael 42

Kent, Constance 65, 70, 89
King, Francis 65
Knoller, Marjorie 33, 35–36
Kouao, Marie Therese 51

Law, Cardinal Bernard 47–48, 90
Lindsey, Gregory 36
Little, Florence 63

McVeigh, Timothy 78
Madonna 25
Manning, Carl 51
manslaughter 11, 14, 35, 85, 89
men 13, 18, 22–26, 30, 76
   violence by 22–23, 26
Meredith, Elaine 34, 90
Moreland, Lesley 78–79
murder 11–14, 16–18, 21–31, 35, 38–39, 47, 50–51, 55, 58, 60, 62, 64, 76–77, 78–80, 89–90
   by children 55–67
   by men 22–23, 26–31
   by women 13, 16–19
   of children 49–52

National Crime Victimization Survey 18
neighbors, trouble with 33–43
Neustatter, Angela 81
Nicholson, Lorraine 25–26
Nist, Tim 28–30
Noe, Marie 52
Noel, Robert 35

Parker, Pauline 55, 63–64, 89
Partington, Marian 80
pedophiles 45, 47, 90
Perry, Anne 55, 63–64, 89
pets, dangerous 35–36
poison pen letters 34
prisons 24, 36, 55, 70, 74, 79, 89
punishments 59, 70

rape 18, 22, 30, 47, 49, 63
rehabilitation 55, 59, 70, 72, 74, 76–79
Rocha, Danny 28
Roman Catholic Church 47
Rule, Ann 27

sadism 47, 49
Sant, Tracey 26
satanic abuse 90
schools, shootings in 65–66
Scully, Julie 28–31, 90
sexual assaults 18, 24, 45, 63
Simpson, O.J. 24, 89
Skiadopolous, George 28–29
Smith, Sharon 36
Smith, Susan 50, 89
stalkers 24–26, 90
Stanton, Bernard 42

Tarnower, Dr. Herman 16–17, 89
Tate, Lionel 59–60, 74, 90
Thompson, Robert 59, 77, 89
Thornton, Sara 13–14, 89
Tinning, Marybeth 52
Tyson, Mike 24–25, 62, 89

Venables, Jon 59, 76–79, 89
Violence Against Women 24, 75, 89, 91

Washington, Desiree 24
West, Fred 47, 49, 80, 89
West, Rosemary 47, 49, 80, 89
women 8, 13, 16, 18, 21–24, 26, 30, 47–49, 52, 75, 89, 91
   infanticide by 52
   legal discrimination against 13
   murder by 13, 16–19, 47, 49
   murder of 18, 26–28, 30–31
   in prison 13, 52, 73
   violence against 22–24
   violence by 13

Yates, Andrea 50, 90
Young, Graham 61, 89

PICTURE CREDITS

Front Cover: Christian Martínez Kempin/iStock

Picture Credits: 5, Ondrooo/iStock; 10, ruskpp/Shutterstock; 12, KatarzynaBialasiewicz/iStock; 14, Topham Picturepoint; 14, Topham Picturepoint; 15, Topham Picturepoint; 16, Everett Collection/Newscom; 19, Topham Picturepoint; 20, Corbis; 22, Topham Picturepoint; 23, Corbis; 24, Topham Picturepoint; 25, Topham Picturepoint; 25, Topham Picturepoint; 26, Corbis; 27, St Petersburg Times/ZUMAPRESS/Newscom; 29, Corbis; 31, Popperfoto; 32, Popperfoto; 35, Topham Picturepoint; 37, JWR/iStock; 38, Topham Picturepoint; 40, Topham Picturepoint; 41, Steven Paul Pepper/Shutterstock; 44, Corbis; 46, vita khorzhevska/Shutterstock; 48, Popperfoto; 49, PA Photos; 50, Popperfoto; 51, Topham Picturepoint; 54, Topham Picturepoint; 57, Corbis; 58, TODAY/REX/Newscom; 60, Corbis; 62, Topham Picturepoint; 64, Topham Picturepoint; 66, PA Photos; 69, Topham Picturepoint; 71, Topham Picturepoint; 72, Topham Picturepoint; 73, Topham Picturepoint; 75, Jodi Jacobson/iStock; 76, Topham Picturepoint; 79, Popperfoto; 80, Popperfoto; 82, Remus Eserblom/iStock; 88, agostinosangel/iStock; 92, OcusFocus/iStock; 94, ejwhite/iStock